The Mysteries of Maria Lionza

A Latin American Musical derived from the legend
and practice of Spiritism with Maria Lionza in Venezuela

With the structural guidance of:

**The Joyful the Glorious and The Sorrowful
Mysteries of the Catholic Rosary**

Ceil Gruessing— November 1999
Written for Charlene Spretnak and The Virgin Mary Class
California Institute of Integral Studies, San Francisco, Ca.

Copyright ©2024 by Cecilia Anne Gruessing, M.A. .

Published by Cecilia Anne Gruessing

ISBN 979-8-9919680-3-4 (softcover)
ISBN xxx-x-xxxxxx-xx-x (hardcover)
ISBN xxx-x-xxxxxx-xx-x (ebook)

All rights reserved. No part of this book may be reproduced or transmitted in any form or by any means, electronic or mechanical, including photocopying, recording, or by any information storage and retrieval system without express written permission from the author, except in the case of brief quotations embodied in critical reviews and certain other non-commercial uses permitted by copyright law.

This book is a work of fiction. Names, characters, places, and incidents are the product of the author's imagination or are used fictitiously. Any resemblance to actual locales, events, or persons, living or dead, is purely coincidental.

Printed in the United States

Cecilia Anne Gruessing, M.A.

INTRODUCTION

The following text is a play called "The Mysteries of Maria Lionza". It is about a goddess/legend of a woman named Maria Lionza, who actually lived. It was originally written for a graduate class about the Virgin Mary, and her migration to various parts of the world. I have dramatized the impact of 15th and 16th century events in Spain that helped transport the "Virgin Mary" to Latin America and particularly Venezuela. I also write about the effects of the Spanish conquest on both the native indigenous and African slaves at that time. The Holy Queen Maria Lionza is in fact one of the many Latin American ambassadora's of the Virgin Mary (like Guadelupe in Mexico) and is the central character of this mystery play.

This work is structured in 15 scenes based on the development of the three- part mysteries in the Catholic rosary. In Act I, I have described the historical circumstances of Maria Lionza's birth as "The Joyful Mysteries". In "the Sorrowful Mysteries" (Act II) I look at the Spanish Conquest of Venezuela, using blatant parallel symbolism of the imasculanization of the Third World male and the exploitation of Latin American resources, to the Crucifixion of Christ and the fear of his magical message of peace. I conflate the crucifixion with the decapitation of a great Venezuelan Indian Chief under captivity, Tamanaco.

Act III, as the "Glorious Mysteries" will portray present day worship of Maria Lionza in Venezuela, and Maria's physical death, her ascent to heaven and her famous Coronation.

Maria Lionza is the queen of "Las Tres Potencias" (the three powers) in Venezuela, where she and the Indian Chief Guacaipuro, and the Afro-Cuban liberator of the Slaves, Negro Felipe, work together in spiritual triumvirate to heal, guide, inspire, and accelerate the evolution of all sentient beings. One cannot help but note this parallel triple concept with the Catholic trinity.

This religious practice has been defined by a practice Alan Kardec calls "Espiritismo" (also called ancestor worship), in which departed ancestors, leaders, and healers, as well as animals, and nature spirits descend into the bodies of mediums (Brujos or Curanderos). They talk, see, and heal through those bodies, while the mediums are "asleep" and out of their bodies. I researched and videotaped this activity for three years, during which I made some very significant relationships with Venezuelan devotees and mediums, and most dramatically, with a huge pantheon of spirits from history. As a choreographer and thespian, I firmly believe that theater and dance grew out of this ancient practice of "ancestor worship" and shamanism. Basically, a good performer has the "spirit", and is so convincing or riveting in their delivery, that you actually believe that the character they are portraying is inside of their body. Again, I declare that the work of Las Tres Potencias and their pantheon of characters is the best theater I have ever seen. I was fortunate enough to have conversations with several of these spirits during all night sessions. My "protector's" name is Tamanaco, a great Indian chief who was part of the resistance to the Spanish Conquest. Maria Lionza herself, ceremoniously crowned me as her god daughter. I am proud of these friendships, difficult as it may be for many to understand.

Maria clearly claims the spiritual hearts of many followers. In Caracas there is a famous statue of her that rivets the imagination, sculpted by Alejandro Colon. Naked and straddling a danza-tapir, a lion/ boar looking animal, Maria raises her arms with fearless energy holding a female pelvis bone high above her head. (*page 1*)

I have enjoyed writing about the Virgin Mary and the Queen Maria Lionza in the theatrical form, because I am truly interested in what they represent as role models for women. I realize the benefits of "Organic Inquiry" amongst primary sources (local publications and musical tapes about prayer and natural cures which I bought on the street). I also credit first-hand experience as a patient of the healing ceremonies with the curanderos, as well as my own artistic intuition and creativity that allowed this work to emerge in this radical style.

This free form expression is especially radical in Act I and II, with the apparitions of the Virgin Mary and her moral disapproval of the imperialistic, Spanish dominion in the new world. I don't believe this has been properly confronted by Catholicism and religious history. The perspective from which the Virgin Mary speaks, predicting the birth of Maria Lionza in the Americas, clearly reflects a collective female voice that has been silent and frustrated for so long over the issues of war and violence. (Why don't Popes straight out condemn all acts of war? Why does the bible speak of military victories in the name of God?) I welcome this opportunity to examine what happened in Latin America with the Spanish Conquest, as I am interested in the subsequent tri-racial cultural mix of their spiritual music and beliefs.

Act III will use the Glorious Mysteries to bring us into modern times with the cult practice of Maria Lionza and her Tres Potencias in Venezuela and on her Mountain sanctuary of Sortes (suerte- luck), in Chivicoa. Here the government has reserved a sacred river and ground for her devotees to practice on national park land. My memories of being inside that world of La Montana de Sortes are still vivid.

Act III also addresses the physical death of Maria Lionza and her ascension to heaven where she continues her work in spirit to this day. This play has been supported by spirit, and it is as artist and shaman that I write it in her behalf as historical fiction.

Thank you for the opportunity to follow my mission as a spiritual artist.

Ceil Gruessing— October 1999— San Francisco, Ca.

BACKGROUND

I have chosen to write in theatrical form, about this Goddess- spirit from Venezuela called "Maria Lionza" with connections to the study of the Virgin Mary and her cult in Spain during the XV and XVI centuries. Several aspects of research were used to write this manuscript, from legends to written material, to primary and secondary source interviews, and personal experience. With this background material, you will have a better idea where this magical, nature-based practice comes from.

Pre-Colombian shamanism and mythology reveals a mother water goddess, YARA, amongst the Northern Amazonian tribes of the Tupari. She is portrayed as a mermaid, accompanied by snakes, who lures a young Indian chief into the water where he becomes initiated by his aquatic intercourse with a Spanish woman. Yara also reveals the importance of the flute, the reeds, and the secret memory of an ancient matrilineal history. Some references say that Maria Lionza was initially called "Yara", born in the province of Yaracuy, before she was given the name Maria.

For many people, Maria Lionza is considered "a myth", legend, or another aspect of the Virgin Mary. There are many different stories of her origin, which generally define her as an indigenous descendent on the paternal side of the Caquetio tribe in

Niragua, the daughter of Chief Guare of Yaracuy, the granddaughter of Chief Chilua and the great granddaughter of Chief Yare. They were all famous leaders and warriors from Venezuelan history. Her mother was Spanish. Folklore has Maria descending from the pre-Columbian goddess Yara, and because of her green watery eyes, she was considered a strange, evil, magical being who had to be sacrificed to a great monster/anaconda from the lagoon to protect the tribe. She escapes this tragedy and survives, to become a mythical goddess and hermit-queen of the jungle and its inhabitants. She was later named Maria to connect her to the Catholic church. The legends vary within these parameters.

In reference books she is also conflated with The Virgin of Coromoto, who is Venezuela's Patron Saint, born the same day, October 12 (also on the day Columbus discovered America, and also called the Dia de la Rasa). Clearly, the church has merged with the indigenous cultures to change history and control the masses.

With a very sincere desire to track down Maria Lionza's real roots as a human being, and to validate my actual conversations with her in spirit regarding her past, I have chosen the most logical of the stories which fits the true history of her birth. Through very grass roots Spanish literature, I have discovered an account of Maria's mother, Princess Ana Carolina del Prado de la Talavera de la Reina, back in 15th century Spain. Despite all the supernatural legends, I have gone with Maria Lionza's authentic, primary source description (by interview), stating that her mother was the daughter of a Royal Spanish Encomendero immigrant couple, and her father was an indigenous Venezuelan Indian, Chief Guare. Her controversial birth in the new Caribbean world as Spanish royalty, mixed with indigenous blood, leads her to become the Queen of The Three (racial) Powers (Las Tres Potencias). This triumvirate legitimized the beginning of the melting pot which exists today between the Spanish Castilians, the West Africans (El Negro Felipe) who came with the slave trade, and the Indigenous native Venezuelans (Chief Guacaipuro).

Maria Lionza was destined for "queenship" in the new melting pot world, because of her mixed blood and exotic beauty (green eyes, dark hair) despite fear of her strange blood. She eventually renounced her family and chose to live as a hermit in the jungle with her animals, and became the protectoress of the indigenous peoples, and all living things, providing safety for all endangered species, and condemning murder of any kind upon her land. The Natives eventually accepted her with love despite her clear eyes. The Church wanted her myth to submit to their prescriptions of the Virgin Mary, so the Mission Friars introduced Maria Lionza with obligatory love at an opportune time when spiritual survival from the Spanish conquistadores was only possible through worshipping a mix of their Catholic Mary, the Virgin de Coromoto and their Nature/Earth deities. Maria Lionza provided the connection, although in present day, the church does not acknowledge her and considers her an Indian legend. Maria, however, continues to use Catholic rituals in her prayers and healing.

In 1492 as Spain was taking over many parts of Latin America. After expelling the Moors from their territory, and creating a Catholic Reign of Terror, the powerful rule that King Ferdinand and Queen Isabella created many reasons to migrate to the New Land…..… mainly freedom.

The Cult of the Virgin Mary was very popular in Spain, with many villages having their own "Nuestra Señora", or "Virgin" protectoress who had appeared to some villager and demanded the construction of a church on the spot. In Toledo, Spain there were many Basilicas, Hermitages, and Sanctuaries of "Our Lady" around which regular celebrations and ceremonies took place, often mixing cultures with Arabic traditions, music, and temple architecture leftover from Moorish influences. Yet despite the strength of the Spanish Inquisition, pagan practices still survived, often combining the worship of the earth mother for agricultural fertility and healing purposes, with the benevolent mystique of the Virgin Mary, who promised them salvation if they worked hard, accepted Jesus, prayed the Rosary, and gave to the church.

Outside Toledo, Spain is a hermitage called "Ermito de Nuestra Virgen del Prado de la Talavera de la Reina", constructed sometime in the late 15th century. There Nuns manufactured and painted ceramic pottery by day and called upon the Virgin by night in their sacred groves with songs and dances, incantations, and infusions of herbs, candles, and prayers clearly tied to previous pagan rites.

Here is where Maria Lionza has her maternal Royal Spanish roots, as her mother Ana Carolina del Prado de la Talavera de la Reina was born there to Doña Herminia and Don Juan de la Talavera de Nivar. They came to Venezuela around 1572 to take advantage of the Encomienda System which basically enforced Spanish military law through Spanish entrepreneurs who farmed, mined, or bred animals, and employed/exploited local Indians to work for them in exchange for residence on their own land. Upon coming of age, La Srta Ana Carolina falls uncontrollably in love with a Caquitios Indian Chief named Guare, father of Maria.

Meanwhile, atrocities have taken place all through Venezuela as the conquistadores ruthlessly destroy and exploit villages and tribes. Dozens of famous Venezuelan Indian chiefs go down in the line of duty to their people, including my own protector, el Cacique Tamanaco. Guaicaipuro, being the main native representative in Maria Lionza's trinity court, plays a major role in the final resistance. The invaders were merciless. There are many legends about brave natives who fought to the end, defending their land and people. A smallpox plague brought in by the Spanish also wiped out about two thirds of the indigenous population by 1590. Those natives who remained were now combined with the slave labor created by African immigration into Latin America. Here we meet the other third of Maria Lionza's trinity, El Negro Felipe, a Cuban liberator of African slaves.

Maria de La Onza del Prado de la Talavera de Nivar is born on October 12, 1591, in the deep Yaracuy jungle to hide the fact that she is the illegitimate daughter of a Spanish immigrant, Ana Carolina, and a Venezuelan Indian Chief. Chief Guare's tribe considers her bad luck because of her light-colored eyes, and that her mother comes from royal, Spanish, conquista blood. Ana's parents will not offer inheritance to a half breed child unless the indigenous father becomes a Spanish count under the crown, and a Catholic under the church.

In 1591 there is the legend of the of Ana Carolina meeting a Venezuelan Indian Chief in the river, where they fall in love, and create Maria. Her eventual magical powers are eventually conflated with the Virgin of Coromoto— Protectress of Venezuela, or Patron Saint under the Catholic church. In 1653 a parish was built in Nirgua, over an ancient matrilineal sacred site, called "La Parroquia de Nuestra Señora Maria de la Onza del Prado de la Talavera de la Reina", where she was conceived.

According to channeled material (Santiago de Jesus Rodriguez Moreno) Maria's mother Ana, puts a Negra Hamurapi in charge of Maria while she grows up in the jungle enveloped by nature, insisting that she must be simultaneously trained in the catechism of the Catholic Church. The mother and father promise to return for the baby Maria, after Ana Carolina formally marries Guare in the church. Maria develops supernatural powers in the wild, including particular healing qualities acquired from the Yaracuy River water, and the ability to talk to animals. She takes her name, Maria de la Onza from the onza (lion), which she rides, also called a danta, or a tapir. She dedicates herself to nature and all living things. The plight of the natives against the Spanish becomes her reclusive fight, to maintain her sacred mountain where the natives could take refuge from the Spanish conquerors. It is recorded in Ponce de Leon's journals that he met with her and that HE gave her the name Maria de la Onza del Prado de la Talavera de Nivar, in hopes of winning her back over to the Spanish Monarchy by reclaiming her blood. But she refused and condemned the barbaric slaughter of the native Venezuelan people and the African Slaves, despite her familial connection to the Spanish conquistadores.

Maria takes on the central role of her Trilogy platform of the Three Races, or the Three Powers (Las Tres Potencias or Poderosos) by joining the spirits of Chief Guaicaipuro, and the Great Liberator of the slaves, Negro Felipe. She translates the Christian trilogy of the Father, Son, and Holy Ghost into a fusion of the African, European, and indigenous powers with her prayers, and takes refuge in nature. Here she reigns, allowing no murder of any kind, incorporating more and more courts of spirits.

Maria also is a virgin, despite the attentions of a Spanish soldier, who was madly in love with her, whom she had to reject because she felt emotionally scarred by her own people's selfish and opportunistic ways. She was ashamed to be instrumental in any way for the violence of this Spanish imperialist bloodline. She could only devote herself to nature and healing, and the protection of the humble, subaltern population who had taken her in.

According to Angelina Pollak-Eltz (1987), who is a leading, published scholar on Maria Lionza's cult, the first center under her name was opened in the early 1900s in Caracas by a known curandero and espiritista (healer and trance medium). The cult grew in popularity during the twentieth century amongst the lower class. Moreover, the Venezuelan Dictator General Gomez (1908- 1935), was a devotee of the practice, and also had a mistress who was a priestess of the cult. Marcos Perez Jimenez (1950-1958), another Venezuelan Dictator also participated in the practice.

These ideological, fascist regimes brought great support to a distinctive cultural phenomenon that is still part of the Venezuelan identity.

Maria Lionza's cult became very visible in the 1940's, between the wars, and reinforced its roots with the African Yoruban faith called "Santeria", thereby cementing the racial integration of all the aboriginal and Espiritista practices. The government set aside several acres, six hours east of Caracas, in Chivicoa, Yaracuy, as National Park, called "The Mountain of Maria Lionza", or "Sortes" (Suerte - luck). Devotees come on pilgrimages every weekend to bathe in the healing waters of the Yaracuy River, and to pay their respects to Maria Lionza and her pantheon of nature spirits and ancestors. One comes with their "Brujo" and tribe for three days to set up an altar, sleep under the stars, and pray for miracles. Here, spirits will descend into the bodies of mediums, initiates, or sick patients, to heal or transfer messages to the people. Spirits descend through the permission of God and Maria Lionza. One must pray to her first, for her intercession, and endorsement towards a spiritual encounter with a particular spirit whose specialty might resolve their potentially magical connection to Dios Poderoso and be healed. Sacred space, altars, candles, flowers, music, cigars (tobaccos or hache), baths, and offerings are blessed and conjured to supply truth and abundance, health and love, happiness, and understanding as part of the performance package.

Because I actually studied this practice for three years, I want to convey the mystical aspects of the experience through dramatic events connected to my personal, experiential knowledge. There was also a limited amount of academic information written about the cult. Most of my research, including religious Spanish History in the XV and XVI centuries, is my attempt to ground the story. I have intuitively constructed this script around my own personal acquaintance and interviews with this Holy Queen Mother Maria, and what she told me about her family history.... as well as my experiences witnessing the descent of many spirits under her wing in Venezuela. The Spanish conquest is not mystical and is unpleasantly necessary to the story as history marches on in patriarchal audacity. The chosen sequence of theatrical and musical events delivers what I consider to be a mythic, and folkloric dedication to Maria Lionza and to the Virgin Mary.

It is a pity the great archaea-mythologist Maria Gimbutas did not get to do her research in Latin America. Her Matrilineal/ Goddess formula tends to fit into many of the symbols of birds, chevrons, triangles, and snake designs, left by South and Central American Neolithic ancestors and shamans. This includes findings by Colombus of female clay idols. Goddesses of the maternal waters are also predominant and filter down to present day mother cult folklore all over the Central and South American continent. And what remains in 21st century, subaltern Latino culture is still the solace of a Queen/Mother/Goddess, who loves every living thing, and embraces the rich as well as the sick and poor. Come to her for love, for forgiveness, for healing, in poverty and abundance, in happiness, or death. Learn how to be humble and pray, to recite the rosary, to confess your sins, and the Queen Mother will always listen.

From my personal experience of being in Maria Lionza's presence, hearing her sing the Ave Maria in the bodies of mediums, watching her sip red wine, listening to her wisdom and compassion, being humbled by her blessing of ceremonial Coronation, and being ordained as her Goddaughter, I am humbled by all the warmth and incredible magic. I was finally embraced for my spiritual merit in her court. I am truly honored by the experience and knowing and believing in the actual previous earthly existence of Maria Lionza, enables me to validate her practice. Again, I must declare, that it was the best "theater" I have ever seen in my life. For these reasons, I embody her in the medium of theater, which was born of the rituals of the Ancient Goddess. I thank you Oh Holy Mother, Queen and Saint, Goddess and Virgin, Maria Lionza.

Ceil Gruessing
1999, San Francisco, Ca.

SCENE BREAKDOWN

ACT I

THE JOYFUL MYSTERIES

1. **THE ANNUNCIATION**— An indigenous Amazonian shaman calls the Goddess of the Waters, Yara to heal a barren woman. Yara announces the birth of a warrior and promises the later birth of a Goddess savior. (1480) .... *page 16*

2. **THE VISITATION**— (Outskirts of Toledo, Spain, 1580) The Apparition of the Virgin del Prado de la Talavera de la Reina at a Nun's hermitage (by the same name), who blesses Anna Carolina del Prado de la Talavera as the future mother of Maria Lionza, Goddess of Peace .... *page 19*

3. **THE NATIVITY**— 1591— Anna Carolina falls in love with a Venezuelan Chief Guare, and they conceive "Yara/Maria" within their polarity................................. *page 25*

4. **THE PRESENTATION**— September 1591 — Making proper birth arrangements for a problematic half-breed... *page 27*

5. **FINDING THE BLESSED CHILD**— Maria del Prado de la Talaverra de la Reina (eventually known as Maria Lionza) is born on October 12, 1591 in sacred waters under the vigilance of the Virgin of Coromoto (Patron Saint of Venezuela often identified with Maria Lionza) .... *page 32*

Cecilia Anne Gruessing, M.A.

ACT II

THE SORROWFUL MYSTERIES

1. **THE AGONY IN THE GARDEN**— (1493—Toledo, Spain)—
   The Virgin Mary observes High Holy Mass
   with disgrace as Queen Isabella, King Ferdinand,
   Christopher Colombus, Tomas de Torquemada,
   and Pope Sixtus celebrate the Inquisition and
   the Conquest of the New World .... *page 39*

2. **THE SCOURGING AT THE PILLAR**— 1490's— "Fields of Blood"
   — A "Conquista Ballet, abstractly danced to the
   formal verbal declaration of domination from
   King Ferdinand and Queen Isabella to the
   Indigenous peoples of the New World .... *page 43*

3. **THE CROWN OF THORNS**— (1580)
   Mary appears on an "Encomienda— Mission"
   for captured natives and African slaves run by
   "Encomendros" and Friars - to witness their
   humiliating exploitation as prisoner/workers .... *page 45*

4. **CARRYING THE CROSS**— Mary watches the
   persecution of the great Venezuelan
   Chief Tamanaco as a gladiator in front
   of his own tribe .... *page 54*

5. **THE CRUCIFIXION**— The Transformation
   — Mary returns the decapitated body of Tamanaco
   to the Goddess Yara and her primordial waters.
   Maria Lionza emerges on her "onza" (tapir) to resist
   the Spanish Conquest into the 17th century .... *page 55*

ACT III
THE GLORIOUS MYSTERIES

1. **The Resurrection—** Semana Santa, A Spiritual Session in Catia, Caracas, Easter, 1995 .... page 63

2. **The Ascension—** Pilgrimage to Maria Lionza's Mountain of Sortes; from Caracas to Chivicoa, Yaracuy— May, 1995 .... page 81

3. **The Descent of the Spirit—**Tongues of Fire and the "trabajos" of the Brujos— Maria Lionza's Altar high atop Sortes .... page 90

4. **The Assumption—** FLASHBACK/Transport to Maria's last living day in Nirgua, Yaracuy, August 15, 1653 .... page 108

5. **The Coronation—** October 12, 1995. Dia de la Raza— Maria Lionza's Birthday in Sortes —A Celebration of her Love and Wisdom .... page 115

Cecilia Anne Gruessing, M.A.

ACT I—

THE JOYFUL MYSTERIES

Characters

- **Tupari Shaman**— Pre-Columbian witchdoctor
- **Native Woman**—Young woman trying to become pregnant
- **8 native priestesses**, dancers
- **Yara**— Pre-Columbian Goddess of the waters, origin Brazil
- **8 Spanish nuns**— 16th century
- **8 humble Spanish pilgrims**
- **Doña Herminia del Prado de la Talavera**— wealthy noble— 30
- **Don Juan del Prado de la Talavera**– wealthy merchant/husband
- **Ana Carolina del Prado de la Talavera**— 12-year-old daughter
- **Ana Carolina**— 27
- **Sister Fe**
- **Sister Caridad**
- **Sister Esperanza**
- **Caquetio warrior Chief Guare**— 28
- **La Negra Hamurapi**— 30 ish African slave nanny
- **Black Virgin Mary**
- **Virgin of Coromoto**— same as Mary

Scene 1— The Annunciation
— Pre-Colombian Ceremony invoking YARA, 1480

There is darkness. In the distance we can hear the approaching sound of a reed flute and a drum. The performance area becomes illuminated with the entrance of an aboriginal, Tupari shaman carrying a torch, followed by "the patient" (a young woman), and a string of women who spiral into a circle and begin to sing and dance as the Shaman prepares his sacred ground. A three-tiered universe is portrayed with the ceremony taking place on the earthly plane, which is suspended between the celestial vault (looks like an inverted bowl), and the subterranean waters, and connected by a large central tree (the axis mundi) and sacred caves.[1] The song about Yara[2] has been passed down into Portuguese even though their original songs were in Tupi.

CANTO da YARA   **(Ronaldo Barbosa)**[3]

Canta e encanta sereia dos lagos	*Sing and enchant mermaid of the lakes*
Yara dos rios	*Yara of the rivers*
Tua beleza e a propria melodia	*Your beauty is a melody in itself*
Brota das aguas e invade a floresta em sinfonia	*Make water bloom and invade nature*
Encanto que surge ao luar	*Enchantment that surges from this place Symphonically*
Que envolve o pesdador	*That involves the fisherman*
Que seduz o navegador	*That seduces the boatman*
E Inspira o chamane	*And inspires the shaman*
Voz sonora infinita	*Infinite sounding voice*
Brasa ou calor	*ember of heat Everything*
Tudo em volta e	*Everything becomes*
Fogo, incenso, fumo e fervor	*fire, incense, smoke and fervor*
Canta minha sereia	*Sing my siren*
Yara dos rios	*Yara of the rivers*
E quando voce para, para, para, para ouvir	*It is when you stop to listen*

E quando voce pensa em voltar	*You think there is no more time*
nao ha mais tempo	
Tudo fica tao distante de voce	*Everything remains so far from you*
O canto de sereia seduziu voce	*The song of the siren seduces you*
Um canto caprichoso seduziu voce	*The capricious song seduces you*

The shaman positions the woman on a mat of leaves near the central tree. He wears tight, feathered, encircling ligatures, or bands on his forehead, upper arms, lower legs, and waist, which enhance his physical power. He shakes his maraca to clear the area around the patient. He begins to play his flute, when the women finish their song to YARA, echoing the melody of their song. He then uses the flute as a straw on the top of the patient's head, and then on her navel.[4] He takes a special wooden spatula and makes himself vomit. Then he positions himself on his "duho", a carved wooden ceremonial seat with the legs of a jaguar, where he will snort the fine, cinnamon colored cohoba powder,[5] and from his hunched "thinker" position, he will call the great Goddess YARA.

Shaman: I, Tupari shaman, call to the forces of the great universe to open the door to this young woman's curse of barrenness. I ask the spirits of nature to lead me to the cause of her imbalance, and to the plant or animal who can cure this disease. Please bring us the power of the great Goddess YARA, whose love and protection the Tupari people cannot live without. Oh, great Goddess of the dark waters, please bless this woman with your presence, your miraculous remedies, your strength and protection, your beautiful fertility, and your all-powerful love. Yara, Yara, Yara . . . .

Kaleidoscopic vision takes over as the Shaman becomes dizzy. The dancers begin to reflect this shift and become jaguars who guide the Shaman into his own feline body language and direct him to a plant. Then, the guaraguao eagle arrives— a celestial bird which takes him through the tree to the celestial heavens where he sings and dances ecstatically with the eagle. And finally, the raw, gypsy-like voice of YARA shatters the ambiance, and the shaman is drawn back to the earth plane, near his patient, flat on his back. On the nearby shoreline, YARA emerges from the subterranean waters with her powerful wailing lament. She is half woman, half fish/anaconda.

YARA: Hello, my people, I am Yara. I am clearly moved by your devotion to my powers. This beautiful woman is physically capable of making a child. The man who is the elected father has not appeased the spirit of a jaguar he killed without permission.

This is forbidden in my world. I cannot permit the entrance of this very important female goddess soul at this time, because the blood is not right.[6] As your protectoress I had hoped that she would carry my natural powers into your village, but I must wait for another virgin mother, whose spirit has no blood stain. I will, however, give your patient, a young boy, who will become a great brave chief named Tamanaco.[7] You will need this great leader, and many others, because there are invaders coming from the other side of the world— white men with arms of fire who will try to destroy you and take your land. They carry a great wooden cross— do not be fooled by this cross, for it is the symbol of your death. We have been blessed by many moons of peace, and now this vision brings me great sadness.
However, there is a peaceful Goddess coming, who will have the blood of many tribes in her veins, and she will come to show the many-colored people how to love one another. But now, I must give your people a warrior, of which you will need many, to stand up to the great white man.

Now, bring me the young woman, and let's fill her up.

Yara breaks into more of her wailing lament, which is accompanied by the sound of rain, water and waves. The shaman brings the patient to Yara who encircles her in the water, with her long, anaconda tail, and the women once again begin to sing and dance for Yara. The young girl begins to dance in the rain, to celebrate her newborn fertility, and the scene ends with a violent storm and the sounds of thunder and lightning.

* * *

Cecilia Anne Gruessing, M.A.

Scene 2— The Visitation
— The Hermitage of the Virgin del Prado de la Talavera de la Reina, 1575
(in the rural outskirts of Toledo, Spain)[8]

A procession of nuns in white habits carrying flowers, enters a monastery garden where there is a colorful fountain made of the old painted Moorish ceramic style brought by the Arabs in the 11th century.[9]

The fountain is at one end of the garden, with a statue of a dark Virgin and child. She has a vivid bleeding heart on her chest. Baby Jesus holds a ceramic globe of the earth in his hand. Pilgrims, who are clearly of the lower class, begin to arrive carrying flowers. They have come from the village in a long procession including singers and dancers, and a few bulls.[10]

CON FLORES A MARIA[11]

Venir y vamos todos	*We are all coming and going*
con flores a porfia	*with intended flowers*
con flores a Maria	*with flowers for Maria*
que Madre Nuestra es	*who is Our Mother*
1. De nuevo aqui nos tienes	*Once again you have us, purest virgin,*
purisima doncella mas que la luna	*purer than the beautiful moon,*
bella, prostrados a tus pies. (2x)	*prostrated at your feet.*
2. Venimos a ofrecerte las flores	*We come to offer you flowers from this*
de este suelo, con cuanto amor y	*soil with so much love and longing*
anhelo, Señora, Tu lo ves (2X)	*Señora, you see this.*

The pilgrims encircle the fountain around the Virgin, leaving their flowers. They begin to pray, kneeling with their rosaries, blessing themselves with the holy water.[12] They begin to recite their prayers.

"Por la senal de la Santa Cruz, de nuestros enemigos libranos, Señor Dios nuestro. En el nombre del Padre, y del Hijo, y del Espiritu Santo. Amen

ACTO DE CONTRICION— Yo confieso antes de Dios poderoso y antes de ustedes, hermanas, que he pecado mucho de pensamiento, palabra, obra y omision; por mi culpa, por mi culpa, por mi gran culpa. Por eso ruego a santa Maria, siempre virgen, a los angeles, a los santos, y a ustedes, hermanas, que intercedan por mi antes de Dios nuestro Señor.

AVE MARIA— Dios te salve, Maria, llena eres de gracia, el Señor es contigo; bendita tu eres entre todas las mujeres, y bendito es el fruto de tu vientre, Jesus. Santa Maria, Madre de Dios, ruega por nosotros los pecadores, ahora y en la hora de nuestra muerte. Amen."

Local spectators, the sick, and miracle seekers are congregating. All begin to sing in.

HYMN TO THE VIRGIN QUEEN (Saint Bernard 1120-40)

"O savior Virgin, Star of the Sea
Who bore for child the Son of Justice
The source of Light,
Virgin always Hear our praise!

Queen of Heaven who have given
Medicine to the sick, Grace to the devout,
Joy to the sad, Heaven's light to the world

And hope of salvation;
Court royal Special Virgin
Grant us cure and guard

Accept our vows, and by prayers
Drive all griefs away!

(Henry Adams piece)[13]

The Countess Doña Herminia del Prado de la Talavera enters the garden with her young daughter, Ana Carolina del Prado de la Talavera, who is about 12 years old. They are definitely overdressed and unexpected for the night's dark mysteries. A nun greets her.

Sister Fe: Señora del Prado de la Talavera! We were not expecting you this evening. This is a service for the sick and poor. Is there something I can do for you?

Doña Herminia: I'm very sorry to surprise you like this sister, but I believe that my daughter is very ill, and the physicians cannot determine the source of the disease.

Sister Fe: What are her symptoms?

Doña Herminia: It is some kind of epilepsy they say, that comes on when she is tired, and lately it seems to be occurring more and more often. She seems tortured by images of hellish worlds where people are being slaughtered like animals. I am so afraid it is consuming her. Look at her, my poor darling, she is so exhausted and confused, what with our move to the new world coming next week. I can't bear to take her on the boat like this. Sister, please help me. She is such a precious soul, and our only child who must carry on our name in Venezuela.

Sister Esperanza: We all love sweet Ana Carolina, and it saddens my hearts to hear of this affliction. Let me take her to the Virgin.

Doña Herminia waits in the background, while Ana Carolina joins the others lighting candles around the dark Virgen del Prado de la Talavera de la Reina.[14] *They begin to sing another prayer to Mary, when some of the sick break down and weep uncontrollably in their petitions for healing and happiness. The nuns invoke the presence of spirit with a libretto style prayer, overlapped by individual prayers and petitions for healing.*

ANCIENT PRAYER TO THE VIRGIN[15]

We turn to you for protection,	*Pedimos protection*
holy Mother of God.	*Madre de Dios sagrada*
Listen to our prayers	*Oiga nuestras oraciones*
and help us in our needs.	*Ayudanos con nuestros necessidades*
Save us from every danger	*Guardenos de cada peligro*
glorious and blessed Virgin.	*Oh, mi virgin gloria y bendita.*

(PRESENCIA DEL ESPIRITU)[16]

Santa Maria, Madre del Señor	*Holy Mother Mary, Jesus's mother*
Jesus y nuestra	*& ours*
obtennos la presencia vivificante del Espiritu	*Give us the living presence of the spirit*
y la gracia de andar siempre por los caminos de Dios	*and the grace to walk with God*
por tu bondadosa intercesion	*For your blessed intercession*
Consigue que estemos libres	*Continue to keep us free*
de las tristezas presentes	*of the present sadness*
pilgrim # 1: de las acechanzas del enemigo,	*from enemy attacks*
pilgrim # 2: de las flaquezas en la lucha,	*from the scars of life's battle*
piligrm # 3: de la pobreza y el hambre	*from poverty and hunger*
pilgrim # 4: de la plaga y muerto temprano	*from the plague and early death*
Y para cuando seamos convocados por el Padre	*And when we are called by the father*
consigue para nosotros las alegrias sin fin— Amen	*Find us happiness without end. Amen*

A crescendo builds during these passionate requests for help and salvation. Suddenly, Ana Carolina begins to convulse and roll on the floor in front of the statue of the Virgin. Out of nowhere we hear a voice singing Ave Maria. Doña Herminia and the nuns come to Ana's aid, who is faint.

Herminia: Mi hija, que pasa?

Sister Esperanza: Is it just me, or does the air seem fragrant with roses?

Sister Caridad: Dios Mio, the Virgin is crying!!!!

She Points to the statue.

Anna Carolina revives and begins to glow with marvel as she focuses on the weeping statue of Mary. Mary steps out from behind the statue.

Ana Carolina: Mama, she is calling me. She wants me to go to her.

Doña Herminia: Go my child, and listen well, for you are the only one who can see or hear her.

Sister Fe: What does she say Carolina? Why is she weeping?

Sister Esperanza: I swear I smell roses . . . .

Ana Carolina: She says that— *(The crowd freezes)*

Mary *(The statue is replaced by an actress who takes over the light)*:
"I weep over the horrors of the present world. I weep over the lies of the people who themselves forge the weapons of destruction. I weep over the selfish ingratitude of God's children"[17]

Ana Carolina: What have we done Holy Mother?

Mary begins to weave a path among all the frozen pilgrims as she speaks with Ana Carolina.

Mary: Our leaders have gone too far with the Inquisition. Too many people have died unnecessarily, in the name of the church— the Moors, the Jews, the pagans . . . This violence cannot bring peace. And it does not stop.

Ana Carolina: Mother, please tell me what we should do . . .
I am going crazy from the mad killing. I can see these pictures in my nightmares, of these horrible, bloody deaths, of poor innocent brown people!!!
I cannot stand to go to sleep, to see any more of this pain and massacre— this must surely be hell!!

Mary: You are seeing the truth and violent ignorance of the Spanish Conquistadores throughout the New World. Your particular visions are of Venezuela where the men are being murdered, tortured, impaled on sticks. Some are being ripped apart by wild dogs; and the rest of the population will die from smallpox. Teresa of Avila has had similar visions. We have been merciless once again in the name of the cross and my precious Father God. This is why I weep.

Ana Carolina: But holy mother, my queen, can you explain why I must see these tortures? I am going to Venezuela, and I never want to see this.
How can we stop this torture Holy Mother, Blessed Queen? What can I do?

Mary: Sweet child of such purity and innocence, come let me hold you close to my bleeding heart. Now listen child … because your family is moving to America … because of your innocence, you have been chosen to conceive a child by the seed of an indigenous man from the New World. Your daughter will have my heart, and she will be a queen, and a savior for a new Holy Trinity in the New World. She will be miraculously endowed with the understanding and the powers of Mother Nature, through the Goddess Yara of the Waters, in the deep Amazon jungles of the new world. Remember my words, for your road will be that of an "eccentric" pioneer for peace in the New World where crossbreeding will clearly be considered taboo. But your child will be one of my saints. I promise you. And you must promise me that she will be brought up under the doctrine and morality of the Catholic Church and our Lord Jesus Christ as you have been trained.

Ana Carolina: I promise to do as you say, Mother. Thank you for your blessings. I will honor your wishes and pray the rosary daily. Please stay with me always. *Ana Carolina reaches up and dries Marias tears with her hair.*

Mary: I will come through you, my child. And I have removed your sensitivity to the pain of the Conquista, so that you can cultivate peace with your influence as a citizen of the Spanish Crown. This act is endorsed by my son, as he well knows the torturous pain of his own death and wishes that no one suffers oppression ever… anywhere… in his name.

Ana Carolina: Oh Glory Glory!!!!!

The crowd comes to life: HALLELUJAH!!!!!

Ana Carolina*: Announcing to the crowd as it recovers from a mystical sleep...*
The Holy Mother will now heal all of you in this hour.

Doña Herminia embraces Anna Carolina.

Doña Herminia: In the name of God, Holy child, tell me what happened?

Ana Carolina: I have been healed Mother, and I cannot wait to set foot in the New World. We must leave these people to their privacy with the holy Mother. Let us go.

Doña Herminia: Of course, darling.

Somewhat awestruck, she makes the sign of the cross to the Virgin, thanks the nun, and leaves with Ana Carolina. The Nuns sing a reprise of the last song to the Virgin as others take their prayers on their knees, and line up for the magic spot to be seen by the Virgin.

Scene 3— The Nativity
— The Conception of Yara/Maria

This scene is performed entirely to music as a dramatic ballet between ANA CAROLINA, at the age of 27, and a young Caquetio indigenous warrior named GUARE.[18] Cacique Guare enters with his band of hunters and they come to the river where they do many things— fish, make fire, fashion arrows, eat, and nap. Ana Carolina is proper and mature now, yet still overdressed for a hot day in the Venezuelan jungle, fanning herself vigorously to keep off flies and beads of sweat. She sees the river and decides immediately to disrobe and take a refreshing dip in the cool waters.

Ana Carolina immerses herself in a tranquil river pool and begins to sing out loud sonnets to the Moon Goddess.

> "Benevolent nourisher; great Nature's key
> Belongs to no divinity but thee . . .
> Thine is the task to unlock the virgin

**With births you sympathize, though pleased to see the numerous offspring of fertility.
When racked with nature's pangs and distress
Sex invokes thee, as the soul's sure rest ..."**[19]

Cacique Guare wakes up and sees this beautiful, strange, white woman in the river, and assumes it is YARA. She is beautiful, and he is overtaken by her aquatic bliss. Surely this is Yara, Goddess of the Waters. He calls to her and moves closer to a rock, where he sits and further observes her. Ana is startled, yet not naked.

Her song ceases, and he asks her to continue. She gets out of the water, and he begins to sing madly, calling out like a fool on the rock in his native tongue, although this is **Hildegard Bingen***.*

> **Guare:** "Hail to you, O greenest, most fertile branch!
> You budded forth amidst breezes and winds
> in search of the knowledge of all that is holy.
> When the time was ripe
> your own branch brought forth blossoms.
> Hail greetings to you!
> The heat of the sun exudes sweat from you like the balsam's perfume.
> In you, the most stunning flower has blossomed
> and gives off its sweet odor to all the herbs and roots,
> which were dry and thirsting before your arrival.
> Now they spring forth in fullest green!
> Because of you, the heavens give dew to the grass,
> the whole Earth rejoices; Abundance of grain comes from
> Earth's womb and on its stalks and branches the bird's nest.
> And, because of you, nourishment is given to the human family and
> great rejoicing to those gathered round.
> And so, in you O gentle Virgin is every fullness of joy".[20]
>
> I want you beautiful woman!!!

Ana Carolina*: (laughing)* I know!!!

He dives into the water and arrives at her side in seconds flat.

Guare: You are like my water Goddess Yara. Do you know her?

Ana: No, I don't believe so … do you know my Goddess Maria?

Guare: No, but I want to know you.

They dance subtly at first, circling each other like animals. They are so different, but she likes his strength, his innocence, his ardent focus. He is mystified by Ana; he likes to look at her, to smell her, to laugh at her ways, and to marvel at her elaborate clothing, used to frame, conceal, and display all parts of her magnificent porcelain body. He lifts her, and she likes it. He carries her into the water, and an underwater duet begins, where they symbolically release and consummate their love through a sacramental marriage duet, which ends in a not so immaculate conception in the water.

Scene 4 — The Presentation and Purification — The Half breed Savioress needs a "manger"

Doña Herminia and Don Juan del Prado de la Talavera are sitting at either ends of an elegant European lunch table in their hacienda in Tocuyo, Venezuela. The Negra Hamurapi is serving them. 1591.

Don Juan: I cannot stay long for this meeting. There are problems with the Indians and the new slaves at the Encomienda[21] mission and I must go resolve them.

Doña Herminia: Juan, we must resolve this very major problem with Ana Carolina and her, her ….

Don Juan: Her fiancé, Herminia … Yes, I know. They will be married as soon as I can arrange for his title with the Queen as "Conte de la Coruna."

Herminia: And meanwhile … their child will be born any minute and we will be the shame of the pueblo .. I can't even imagine what the child will look like.

Juan: She will look like you and me and these pagan savages and there is nothing we can do about it.

Herminia: Please Juan, I don't feel she is safe to have the child here. Everyone is waiting like flies on honey to find out who the father is.

Ana Carolina enters very pregnant, hot and bothered.

Herminia: There you are my child. How are you feeling this afternoon?

Ana Carolina: Oh mother, I feel like I'm carrying the world, and there is absolutely no position in which I find myself comfortable. Have you seen William yet?

Juan: Oh, are we calling him William now? What happened to El Grand Cacique Guare del Tribu Caquetios?

Ana Carolina: This is the name we've decided upon.

Juan: And what will you name your son?

Ana Carolina: Father, it is a girl, as the Virgin told me herself, whom we shall call Maria in her honor.

Herminia: The Virgin spoke to her at the hermitage in Spain and told her that she would carry a Goddess in her womb.

Juan: Maria del Prado de la Talavera de la Reina . . . Well, I guess we can't argue with the Virgin Mary, can we???

Guare enters wearing European clothing in awkward fashion. Ana Carolina runs to greet him.

Guare: I'm sorry I'm late. My tribe has moved deeper into the forest near the healing waters of the Yaracuy River[22]. I have been with our curandero who believes these waters hold a remedy for the smallpox. My mother is sick along with so many others in my tribe.

Ana Carolina: Oh, I am so sorry William, for I do so much want her to meet our baby. I want to go there and meet your mother. Feel her William, she is always dancing; she will be strong like you.

Guare: And beautiful like you, my flower.

Herminia: Please sit down and join us for lunch William.

Juan: So, how are your workers doing in the mines William?

Guare: I'm sorry sir, but I cannot speak the truth.

Juan: You can speak the truth with me Guare.

Guare: Sir, they don't understand how the white man can take their land away from them, and then make them work for you, while you take the profit. They are also discouraged by the plague that has killed so many of us, and they do not like your God.[23]

Juan: That's enough Guare ... Heathens!!! What about progress? Do these people want to be stuck in the past forever?

Ana Carolina: Must we discuss this now Father??

Herminia: Yes, let's talk about the baby.

Ana Carolina: Yes, our precious, special child ... I cannot wait to hold her.

Herminia: Ana, your father and I feel that it would be safer for you to have the child outside the village. *Silence strikes the table.*

Ana Carolina: But why Mother?

Herminia: Because you are not married, and this is not good for the family or the child.

Ana Carolina: But mother, our marriage status will not dictate the birth of this baby. How much longer can we keep our love a secret?

Guare: Excuse me Ana ... *(addressing Juan)* I want very much to marry your daughter Sir. But I have also been warned about bringing a child with clear eyes into my tribe.[24] (fn salazar pg55) They believe it is bad luck, and they have already moved farther into the jungle near the Yaracuy River, to escape your people. I am in a difficult position, but I want to do what is right for the child.

Juan: And how do you think our people will feel about it? You cannot marry my daughter unless you become a Catholic and that's final.

Ana Carolina: He is the father of my child and that's enough marriage for me. I love him.

Herminia: Ana, think what you are saying! We are civilized remember.

Guare: I can take Ana to a special place in Yaracuy, in the jungle, high on a mountain above my people, where she will be surrounded by nature. There is a small shrine to Yara there where she will be comfortable. *(footnote found on page 31)*

Negra Hamurapi: Señora, I will go with Ana. I am a midwife, and I can care for her and the child there. I have heard of this sacred place.

Juan: I believe this is an excellent solution.

Ana Carolina: Oh Negra, do you think the Holy Mother will watch over us?

Negra Hamurapi: She is with you all the time, as I will be. Do not worry.

Herminia: Oh, what a relief! This surely makes me feel better.

Juan: Then it is settled. William, I will arrange your patronage to the crown at once, and then after the marriage you can bring the child back to Tocuyo, provided of course, that you convert to the Catholic church.

Guare: I am doing what I can to adapt to your culture. Give me time . . . I will take the women to see my mother at daybreak, and then on to the sanctuary. Our child will be born in paradise near holy river waters. This will please the Goddess Yara, and maybe she will bring the rain so that my flower won't be so hot and uncomfortable.

Juan: Ask Yara if she wouldn't mind raining on the crops as well. The farmers are going out of business with this drought.[25] *(He rises from the table to leave)* So now that the baby problem is 'somewhat' settled I must go to the Encomienda and resolve more problems. Please excuse me.

He kisses Anna Carolina, shakes Guares hand, and leaves; Guare and Anna leave.

Negra Hamurapi: Then I shall prepare Lady Ana for the trip Señora?

Herminia: Thank you Hamurapi . . . what would we do without you?

Negra Hamurapi: Señora, this baby has already been blessed by the spirit.

Herminia: You must promise me that the child will be trained in the full Catechism of the church, as Ana was. This is very important to us.

Negra Hamurapi: I understand Señora, and as I have raised Ana, I will raise your granddaughter under the grace of the Holy Mother, and her son, our Lord Jesus Christ.[26]

    Herminia: Amen que se sea.

*In Nirgua, Yaracuy in the 17th century (1653) a parish was founded with the name of "Nuestra Señora Maria de la Onza de Prado de Talavera de Nivar" on the site of an ancient indigenous sanctuary.

http://www.nodo50.ix.org/SODEPAZ/21art8.htm— ARTICULO 8 CUADERNOS N 21 (in Spanish)

The Virgin of Coromoto

Scene 5 — Finding the blessed child in the "Temple" — The Virgin of Coromoto Guanare, Venezuela. in the Ravine near the Tu cupido river- September 8, 1591

Guare, Ana Carolina, and the Negra Hamurapi are walking in the jungle. They come to the river. Ana Carolina is very pregnant, and they have taken a break to water themselves and the horses.

Guare: This is the holy water place, where my people come to pray and heal.

Ana: Can we bathe in the water? I'm so hot, and the water looks so refreshing.

Negra: How I wish it would rain? Feels like months since we've had a drop.

Guare: And the river is low, but high enough to bathe. I will water the horses. Watch out for snakes.

Negra: Señora Ana, let us say a quick prayer, if you wouldn't mind?

Ana: Of course, mi nodriza *(nursemaid)*.

Anna Carolina and la Negra Hamurapi kneel on the riverbank and pray

> **"Soul of Mary, sanctify me.**
> **Heart of Mary, inflame me.**
> **Hands of Mary, support me.**
> **Feet of Mary, direct me.**
> **Immaculate eyes of Mary, look upon me.**
> **Lips of Mary, speak for me.**
> **Sorrows of Mary, strengthen me.**
> **O Mary, hear me**
> **In the wound of the Heart of Jesus, hide me.**
> **Let me never be separated from thee.**
> **From my enemy defend me.**
> **At the hour of death, call me.**
> **And bid me come to thine Immaculate Heart**
>
> **That thus I may come to the Heart of Jesus**
> **and there will the saints praise you**
> **For all eternity." Amen**[27]

Anna Carolina disrobes within 10 seconds and descends in o the water.

Ana: Oh, my baby likes this and so do I. Venga mi Negra, Quita su ropa!

Negra: If you insist dear Ana, I won't decline the invitation in this heat.

Ana: Oh, this is like heaven, I never want to leave this river. O mi Negra, I am just too tired to meet his mother now. Can't we just stay here forever?

Negra: Ana my sweet, you carry his people's blood in your belly, and he wants you to know and like them. Can you blame him?

Ana: Of course not, I love William with all my heart. I hope his mother likes me.

Negra: Ana, your people have killed off most of his people, in one way or another. He is trying to make peace between enemies, and the world sits on his shoulders.

Ana: Well, I've got the world in my womb, and I hope I can get back up on that horse again.

Negra: Señora, I promise to make you comfortable in the mountain shrine.

Ana: Negra, I have never told you of the vision of the Virgin I had in Spain when I was a young girl telling me this would all happen with William. She told me that this would all happen, and that our baby would be a pioneer queen for peace in Venezuela. Santa Maria is with me all the time, and she will come to the shrine on the mountain to bless the child there.

Negra: Yes, I too believe that baby Maria will be a beautiful child with supernatural powers; and I promise you that I will care for her as if she were my own.

Ana: *(sadly)* You promise to hold her close to you a lot, and to sing to her, the way you sang to me, and to teach her the rosary .... you know? ....

Negra: Ana, I know what to do.

Ana: I know you know what to do, and I love you Negra... you always fix everything. God Bless You. Now, can you stop me from weeping?

Hamurapi splashes her face with water and makes her laugh.

Ana: Hamurapi, do you smell roses?

Guare returns from watering the horses and hears a divine female voice singing Ave Maria. He looks deeper into the ravine and sees a blaze of golden burning light rise up, inside which floats the Virgin Mary (As the Virgin of Coromoto) seated on her throne with Jesus on her lap holding a blue ball with a golden cross on it. She is singing and waving the three colored (blue, yellow, red) flag of Venezuela. Guare is spell bound. And the Virgin Mary speaks to him.

Virgin of Coromoto: You must collect your people and leave the forest. Go to the white men in order to be blessed and receive the water on the forehead so as to be able to enter heaven.[28]

She says this to him in his native language. This infuriates Guare. He cannot help but reject her commands.

Guare: Why must you touch every part of our lives? Why can we not worship our own God? Please let me keep what is my own true spirit!!!!!

This shouting causes YARA to arrive as turbulence in the river, bringing on thunder and rain. Ana Carolina begins to scream.

Ana Carolina: Oh Santa Madre, help me, my water has broken.

Negra: Come on hija, push! The river water is warm. This is the way my mother taught me in Africa.

Ana: William, help me! *(she prays)* Dios me salve, Reina, Madre de misericordia, vida, dulzura y esperanza mia............Dios me salve

Guare: *(supporting her)* Look my flower, there they are... Both my Yara and your Maria have come to bless our baby.

Ana: Oh, dulce Santissima Madre, gracias..... gracias... Oh, I feel another contraction!!... Deme sus bendeciones por favor en el nombre del

Padre, Hijo, y Espiritu Santo.

Negra: Come on Ana, push!!! I can see the head. Come on mujer!!

Ana: *(screaming)* Ayuda me MADRE!!!!

Negra: *(quoting yet shouting from the Song of Solomon)* "She brought forth like a strong man with desire, and she bore according to the manifestation . . . And acquired with great power!!!"[29]

Ana: *(letting out a final, award-winning scream)* MADRE!!!!!

Virgin of Coromoto: Tranquila mi hija, Estoy aqui contigo! I am here to protect you and bring light to you and your royal baby. Bendeciones . . . I bring to you a sacred daughter, from my purest heart. This child, Maria, will have her own mission as the Queen of the Three Powers (Las Tres Potencias). This will be her Spiritual trinity in Venezuela for the three races— The indigenous Indian, the African immigrated slave, and the European Spanish settlers. The holy Father blesses her with the powers of the Catholic Church and gives her direct contact with the divine. She will heal and be a Queen of the people. She will be the Patron Saint of Venezuela.[30] And this ravine will forever be a source of healing water for all who touch it. She will be remembered in formal recorded history as The Virgin of Coromoto. I baptize her in the name of the Father, the Son, and the Holy Ghost. *(she disappears, and Ana passes out)*

Despite the rain and thunder, this burning image of the Virgin has riveted the attention of Anna and Guare, as they all sit together in bloody river water. Negra Hamurapi presents them with a beautiful baby girl with black hair and green eyes.

Negra: Ana Carolina, your baby Goddess is here.

Guare: Come back to us Ana, our child is here. *(he revives her)*

Ana: Dios mio, where was I? *She sees the child* ... Oh, Santa Maria. . . . she is just beautiful ...look Guare; she looks like you.

Guare: She has beautiful clear eyes like yours, and her spirit is strong ...Yes.

The clouds clear, and with the sun comes a rainbow. Indigenous voices begin to sing a song to Yara, and Guare's mother arrives with her singing tribe and descends the banks of the river to see the new baby with clear eyes.

> **SONG to Yara**
>
> **Cuenta la leyenda que cerca del horizonte**
> **Vive una reina encanta por la noche**
> **Ella es tan bella que ilumina las estrellas**
> **Fuerte es la magia que transmite su presencia**
> **Son espiritus que cuida tu cammino**
> **Llevandote siempre hacia el bien**
> **Si solo crees ella estara contigo**
> **La Diosa de Yara – Ayudales**   Johans Guevara

Guare begins to rock the baby to the song to Yara, who is passed to his own mother, back to Ana, and then is reluctantly handed to Hamurapi.

Guare's mother: You must go now Guare. Our people will not accept your woman, for her people have been the cause of all our sorrow. And it will take some time for the child with her clear eyes and light skin to be trusted.

Ana: But this is my child, my baby!!!

Negra: It is better that you go now. I will keep my promise to care for her.

Guare's mother: And I will guide her to Yara's sanctuary on the mountain.

Guare carries the reluctant, weeping Ana away and they leave together to return to Tocuyo. Yara appears from the water.

Yara: Oh, joy of all joys, finally I see the fruits of my own soul incarnated in such pure beauty. Oh, my sweet Princess, how you will solve the mystery.

Hamurapi and Yara sing to Maria on the shores of the river.

END OF ACT I

Cecilia Anne Gruessing, M.A.

The Mysteries of Maria Lionza

ACT II—

THE SORROWFUL MYSTERIES— MURDER OF THE INDIGENOUS SPECIES OR THE SPANISH CONQUISTA

Characters

- **Pope Sixtus IV**— Spanish 16th century pope
- **King Ferdinand**
- **King Isabella**
- **Christopher Columbus**
- **Torquemada**— Christian Monk
- **White Virgin Mary**
- **Bartholeme de las Casas**— Spanish Friar
- **Nectorio Maria**— Spanish Friar
- **Captain Pedro Alonzo**— Spanish Soldier
- **Captain Tapia**— Spanish soldier
- **7 Native Indians**
    Including Chief Tamanaco
    Chief Manaure
- **el Negro Felipe**— Liberator of the slaves
- **6 African Slaves**
- **Virgin Mary**— native indgenous blood
- **The female Indian**—Tivisay— daughter of Tamanaco
- **The male Indian**—Terapaima— son of Tamanaco

Cecilia Anne Gruessing, M.A.

Scene 1— The Agony in the Garden
— Holy High Mass— Toledo, Carnival— 1493

A 15th Century Spanish Processional brings Ferdinand, Isabella, Colombus, Torquemada, and the Pope Sixtus IV down the isle of the big basilica. They all kneel in front of the pope while he splashes them with holy water. The congregation is full of members of the court.

O GENITRIX AETERNI— Processional Hymn

**"O bearer of the eternal word, virgin Mary,
what voice, what human tongue can praise you well enough?
You, new star of the sea, window to the lofty heavens,
ladder from earth to heaven, from the lowest to the highest.
You conceived eternity, you gave birth to your parent.
the maker came from what he made,
the creator from the creature."**[31]

**Mary delivers her dialogue as spirit, which only we (the audience/ reader) can see and hear.

Pope: Glory be to the Father and to the Son and to the Holy Ghost. As it was in the beginning, is now, and ever shall be, world without end. Amen.

The Kneeling Three: "Thou shalt sprinkle me, Lord, with hyssop and I shall be cleansed; thou shalt wash me and I shall be made whiter than snow."

Pope: Show us Lord your mercy.

Three: Halleluia!

Pope: And grant us Your salvation.

Three: Halleluia!

Pope: Let us pray. "Hear us Lord, Holy Father, almighty and eternal God; and graciously send your Holy Angel from heaven to watch over, to cherish, to protect, to abide with, and to defend all who dwell in this house. Through Christ our Lord. Amen."[32] *They get off their knees.*

Pope: Ladies and gentlemen, good Catholics, and members of the congregation; we gather here today to celebrate a very important milestone in the history of the Catholic Church on this year 1492. Spain now belongs to the Catholic Church and to no other previous conquerors. And we owe this to the unifying skills of our beloved King Ferdinand and Queen Isabella.
Not only have they reformed the clergy, but they also have united Spain politically through their royal marriage, they have engineered the Reconquista, and they have delivered the Spanish Inquisition all in the name of the Holy Roman Catholic Church. Citizens of Spain, I give you your King and Queen.

Ferdinand: I have just returned from Granada, victorious over the last Moorish bastion in the southeast, marking the end of a nine-year battle which cleanses our land of the Islamic culture for the first time in two hundred years.[33]

Mary's head rolls right off her statue body, and crashes to the floor. The spirit of Mary then appears near the altar, clearly annoyed by the hypocrisy of the situation. An altar boy scrambles to pick it up as the service continues. Mary's dialogue is only heard by the audience.

Mary: Let me tell you it was a blood bath, I was there!

Ferdinand: I am proud to have been part of the diplomacy and military strategy which has achieved this Reconquista. May I present to you your queen, Isabella.

Mary: Get ready for a really big show Ladies and Gentlemen.

Isabella: We are triumphant! We have accomplished our goal. Spain is religiously pure and belongs to the Church and there it will stay in the name of God, the Father, the Son, and the Holy Ghost.

Mary: Pobrecita, she thinks all she has to do is cross herself every five minutes!

Isabella: Our soil is now free from Moors, Jews, gypsies, witches, pagans, and even the Protestants.

Mary: In the name of which God are you free your highness?

Isabella: Remaining "Moriscos" have been given the choice of voluntary exile or conversion to Christianity.[34]

Mary: I don't remember them being offered a choice.

Isabella: We must make room for the many "Conversos" (converted ones) who will be coming into church. And now I would like to introduce you to my most effective prosecutor in this enterprise, Brother Tomas de Torquemada.[35]

Mary: Another misguided, yet opportunist Catholic soul…poor guy.

Torquemada: I have a deeply religious connection to the Catholic church, and I am proud to be working for both the Pope and the Monarchy in this endeavor. I myself descend from a Converso family. I believe that non-Catholics and insincere converts could destroy both our church and country. Over 2000 Jews, Moors, apostates and deviates have already been investigated, punished and converted in the name of our Holy Father.

Mary: Try abducted, burned at the stake, and murdered without trial!

Torquemada: Our tribunal is composed of inquisitors from the finest Franciscan and Dominican orders. The Spanish Inquisition will live on, until every land under Spanish rule prays under our God and accepts Jesus Christ as his savior. Amen

Isabella: Thank you, Brother Tomas. We must also now celebrate our territorial claims in the New World with a few words from the man who is making us rich after placing our Spanish flag in terra firma, a shrewd businessman and brilliant navigator, Admiral Christopher Colombus.

Colombus: America is beautiful!! She is the gold pot at the end of the rainbow! She has been claimed in the name of the Spanish crown, and it is paradise for Spaniards who wish to pioneer for the golden treasure of El Dorado. As far as the natives…

The Mysteries of Maria Lionza

Mary: Wait until you see how he twists this.

Columbus: ……. "they were very friendly. I knew that they were a people who could be more easily freed and converted to our holy faith by love than by force. Our gifts gave them great pleasure and made them so much our friends that it was a marvel to see."[36]

"They will surely become Christians, for they are inclined to the love and service of Your Majesty and of the entire Castilian nation, and they try to help and share with us the things they have in abundance which we need. And they know no religion nor idolatry, except they all believe that the power and the good is in heaven. And they believed very strongly that I came, with these ships and people, from heaven, and with due respect they receive me everywhere, after they lose their fear. And this is not because they are ignorant, rather they are of keen wit, and they are men who sail all those seas, for the good account they give everything is a marvel. Wherever we go, they run from house-to-house shouting, "Come to see the people from heaven". And after they felt secure with us, all of them came, both men and women, for not even the elderly nor the young would stay behind, and all of them would bring something to eat and to drink, which they offered with marvelous love."[37]

Isabella: Ahh Columbus, how Spain treasures your brilliant courage!!

Colombus: Here is a virgin land to behold for all the world. I invite you to join in the splendor. You are welcome to behold all the gold and pearls, strange fruits, exotic herbs we have brought back with us. (*Pause*) Am I the only one who smells roses?

Mary: (*She walks right up to Columbus, even though he can't see her she says:* Yes, a virgin land with innocent people who will now be raped, pillaged, exploited, and murdered, in the name of your God, not mine.

Colombus: Your perfume is divine Isabella . . .

Isabella: (*turning away demurely*) Now Admiral Colombus, we do not want to lose our population entirely to America. After all, España IS the world power now. (*She smiles*) Thank you so much for your contribution to civilization. We'll talk later.

Mary: Congratulations Christopher, you are the inspiration for the Conquistadores bloody imperialism.

Isabella: And now we want to invite the Pope to deliver Eucharist to all the people in the Plaza outside, where we will enjoy the body and blood of Christ in the form of celebratory libations on the day of the "Diablos."[38] Let us count our sins in Carnival celebration!! Let us drink to the blood of Christ . . .

Mary: …. while you drain the blood of all people of color.

Isabella: *(Exiting the church)* …. And to the purity of España!!! VIVA ESPAÑA!!

Mary: Oh, my dear Queen, one day you and I will have to discuss the barbaric consequences of your actions. Forgive me Father for my sarcasm.

Carnival music can be heard from outside, as the church clears. Mary kneels in front of the altar and recites Psalm 42. There is a parade of devil dancers innocently prancing around the altar while Mary prays.

Mary: "Do me justice, O God, and fight my fight against an unholy people, rescue me from the wicked and deceitful human. For Thou, O God, art my strength, why hast Thou forsaken me? And why do I go about in sadness, while the greedy annoy me? Send forth Thy light and thy truth: for they have brought me to Thy holy hill and thy dwelling place." (Psalm 42) Give me the insight and the strength to understand this need for power and territory, and to protect those less powerful. Help me to forgive the sins of these greedy people, and to lead them out of the path of darkness. In your holy name my Father/God, show me the light.

The Devil dancers take over the altar, and Mary leaves. Lights fade.

Scene 2— The Scourging at the Pillar
— T he Conquest of Venezuela

The following scene will be portrayed as a ballet, and not a beautiful ballet. In a few minutes the entire Spanish conquest of Venezuela will be danced dramatically as Spanish soldiers and Indigenous warriors' skirmish in bloody battle. Because of their firearms and horses, the Spanish have the clear advantage, although all of this will be abstracted in a dance confrontation of cultures, emotions, and painful machismo. There is much torturous "scourging at the pillar" which begins the actual crucifixion of the Third World man/woman/culture. Over the music, King Ferdinand and Queen Isabella will recite their message to the Arawak Indians as the battle ensues. Mary will float around blessing the wounded.

(This speech was originally delivered by Colombus to the Indigenous and has been adapted for the King and Queen in the first person.)

Ferdinand: "In the name of myself, King Ferdinand and our Queen Isabella of Spain, conquerors of barbarian nations, we notify you as best we can that our Lord God Eternal created Heaven and Earth and a man and woman from whom we all descend for all times and all over the world. In the 5,000 years since creation, the multitude of these generations caused men to divide and establish kingdoms in various parts of the world, among whom God chose the Pope as the leader of all Mankind, which means admirable and greatest Father, governor of all men. Those who lived at that time obeyed the Pope as Lord and superior King of the universe, and so did their descendants obey his successors and so on to the end of time.

ISABELLA: The late Pope gave these islands and mainland of the ocean and the contents here of to us, the King and Queen, as is certified in writing and you may see the documents if you should so desire.
Therefore, we as your Royal Highnesses are your lords and masters of this land and are acknowledged as such when this notice is posted, and we will be served willingly and without resistance. Many of our religious envoys have already been acknowledged and obeyed without delay, and all subjects unconditionally and of their own freewill are becoming Christians and thus will remain. We receive their allegiance with joy and benignity and decreed that natives be treated in this spirit like good and loyal vassals AND YOU ARE UNDER THE OBLIGATION TO DO THE SAME!!

FERDINAND: Therefore, we request that you understand this text, deliberate on its contents within a reasonable time, and recognize the Church and its highest priest, the Pope, as rulers of the Universe, and in their name, We, the King and Queen of Spain, as rulers of this land, allowing the religious fathers to preach our holy Faith to you. You owe compliance as a duty to the Spanish Crown and our officials will receive you with love and charity, respecting your freedom and that of your wives and sons and your rights of possession and we shall not compel you to baptism unless you, informed of the Truth, wish to convert to our holy Catholic Faith as almost all your neighbors have done in other islands, in exchange for which we have bestowed many privileges and exemptions.

ISABEL: Should you fail to comply, or delay maliciously in so doing, we assure you that with the help of God we shall USE FORCE against you, declaring war upon you from all sides and with all possible means, and we shall bind you to the yoke of the Church and of Their Highnesses; we shall enslave your persons, wives and sons, sell you or dispose of you as the King sees fit; we shall seize your possessions and harm you as much as we can as disobedient and resisting vassals. And we declare you guilty of resulting deaths and injuries, exempting the Crown. We hereby request that legal signatures be affixed to this text and pray those present to bear witness for us . . ."[39]

The choreography ends with lifeless Indians signing papers. Mary is visibly overwhelmed and sings a lament.

Scene 3 — The Crown of Thorns— Las Encomienda/Missiones

In a crude monastery in El Tocuyo near Barquisimetro, Venezuela in 1572 there is a statue of Mary standing on one side, and a sculpture of Jesus carrying the cross with his Thorn of Crowns on the other side of the altar.

Bartholeme de las Casas[40] and Nectorio Maria[41] are two Friars whose duty it is to civilize the Indians and the African Slaves regarding clothing, behavior, and the ways of the church, feed them, and send them to manual labor everyday with their "Encomendros". Bartholeme is playing a passionate hymn to Mary on a humble organ, while Nectorio Maria arranges the benches for their new conquered students.

Bartholemew sings in romantic bliss, a song to Mary

The Mysteries of Maria Lionza

IN HER PATHS by Francis Thompson

> **"And she has trod before me in these ways!**
> **I think that she has left here heavenlier days.**
> **And do I guess her passage, as the**
> **skies of Holy Paradise turn deeply holier,**
> **And, looking up with sudden new delight,**
> **One knows a seraph-wing has passed in flight**
> **The air is purer for her breathing,**
> **Sure!**
> **And all the fields do wear the beauty fallen from her;**
> **The winds do brush me with her robe's allure,**
>
> **Tis, she has taught the heavens to look sweet,**
> **and they do but repeat**
> **The heaven, heaven, heaven of her face!**
>
> **The clouds have studies going from her grace!**
> **Essence of old, essential pure as she**
> **For this is that Lady, and none other**
> **the man in me calls "Love"**
> **— the child calls "mother."**[42]

(IN HER PATHS by Francis Thompson

At a very passionate point in the music, the monastery door flings open, just violently enough to disturb the revelry Bartholemew has evoked in the sanctuary. A "Capitan Pedro Alonzo"[43] *escorts a string of seven natives into the room. Their hands are tied, they are barely dressed, smeared with warpaint, they are angry, and they are told to sit.*

Capitan Alonzo: *(shouting)* Sientense!!! you savage!!! Do you even know what a chair is?!!

They are mad, but they sit. One in particular (Cacique Tamanaco), is very rebellious.

Nectorio: That's quite all right Captain, we'll take it from here.

Capitan Alonzo: No, I don't trust this one. *(He indicates Tamanaco)*

Bartholeme: I have an idea, let's start with the uniform. *(He passes out Monks robes which they put on)* OK one for everybody. Nectorio, will you please hand out the crosses? Thank you . . . OK, now let's teach them how to do "The Sign of the Cross." *(He holds up the cross against his chest, and encourages them to imitate)* OK, follow me guys: The Father, The Son, and The Holy Ghost. Amen. Shall we do that again? *(It is repeated until they all get it)*

Nectorio: Very good, gentlemen.

Captain Alonzo: What seems to be this one's problem? *He indicates Tamanaco who is not participating, so the captain must force a robe on him, and stuffs the cross into his hands. Tamanaco is furious.*

Tamanaco: First you rape my land, then you kill my brothers with your firearms, next you take our women prisoner, and now you want me to pray to your God. What kind of God is this? You are crazy!! *(He spits) I* will kill you too!!

Captain Alonzo: I should dismember you right here— right now.

Bartolome: Please Captain Alonzo, we are in God's house.

Captain Alonzo: Tamanaco's the big chief…. the big strong, hold out tough guy, Cacique Tamanaco. *(He addresses Tamanaco)* I remember when you charged our men with conch horns.[44] *(Imagining himself there lustfully)* Then we responded, and your men were confused. *(addresses the others)* But then Tamanaco, gathering new inspiration from his men's unexpected disorder, provided gallant resolve and, with macana (machete) in hand, maintained the combat against that large number solely through his vindictiveness . . . So! That was then . . . How strong are you now Tamanaco? Let's you and I step outside for a while OK Chief?

Captain Alonzo and Tamanaco leave, and a string of African Slaves enters, all tied up. El Negro Felipe is among this group.[45]

The Africans are then lined up by Spanish Captain Tapia[46]. They pass out robes and crosses.

The Indians are looking at the Africans, and the Africans are completely overwhelmed. Bartholeme begins the introduction to a marching Hymn. Nectorio tries to lead the singing.

**Onward Christian soldiers,
Marching off to war . . .
With the cross of Jesus,
Going on before . . .
Christ the Royal Master
Leads against the foe
Marching into battle,
see those banners flow.**

The entire scenario becomes a farce, as the Natives and the Africans become more and more stunned by the experience. The effects are comical, yet tragic. Especially when Captain Alonzo returns with a beaten up Tamanaco.

Nectorio: I think that's enough exercise. Let's teach them the table manners.

Tables are pulled up, napkins and spoons are presented, and a fabulous soup which everybody likes. While they are on the soup line, they check each other out, and fumble with tables, chairs, spoons, and napkins. The Negro Felipe is kind and teaches some of the Natives how to use the spoon.

Negro Felipe: If I can teach Guaicaipuro how to drink from a glass, I can teach you how to sip soup!! *(they all sit down)*

Native Manaure: Do you know about Guaicaipuro?

Negro*: (pausing)* I guess the drum didn't get this far.

Bartholeme: Now we are all going to recite the Ave Maria . . . All together now, repeat after me, line by line.

The captain and the monk are now both on behavior modification detail, to force and teach them everything, including not to eat before they pray.

The Ave Maria - in Spanish

> **Dios te salve, Maria**
> **Llena eres de gracia**
> **El Señor es contigo**
> **y bendita Tu eres**
> **Entre todas las mujeres**
> **y bendito es el fruto**
> **de tu vientre, Jesus**
> **Santa maria, madre de Dios**
> **ruega por nosotros, los pecadores**
> **ahora y en la hora de nuestra muerte.**
> **Gracias Madres, por nuestra pan de cada dia ….**
> **En el nombre de Dios Poderoso, el Hijo,**
> **y el Espiritu Santo. Amen**

Manaure: Negro … tell me what happened to Guacaipuro …

Negro Felipe: I'll tell you later amigo.

Manaure: I must hear now, please ……………… Guacaipuro was like a brother to me.

Captain Tapia— He's finally dead!! That's what!! El Grand Cacique Guaicaipuro is dead!! I was there when we ambushed him, I heard his final words. We finally had him outnumbered and surrounded.

Manaure: Hey, Guaicaipuro was the greatest warrior in our land. He organized up to 2000 warriors under his command at a time. He was invincible!!!!

Negro Felipe: Listen hombre, I heard that Guaicaipuro fought to the end. I heard that he pulled out a sword he had taken over from Juan Rodriguez, and with 22 men, he held off the entrance to his village. The whole tribe flanked to his aid, wielding their macanas *(macetes)*. Most of them perished, and there was much lamenting and confusion until the soldiers, weary of the barbarian's defense, threw a firebomb into his house. As it began to spread, Guaicaipuro came to the door of his burning village and screamed:

GUAICAIPURO appears

Guaicaipuro: "Ay Spanish cowards! Because you lack courage to force me to surrender, you use fire to defeat me. I am the one you seek, Guaicaipuro, who never feared your haughty race. Since I am now in this position, though, kill me, and through my death be free of the terror I inspire in you."[47]

There is silence

Negro Felipe: And there he died by the sword of the Spanish invaders on his own land along with his last 22 warriors.

Captain Tapia: Are you trying to start trouble too?

Negro Felipe: My name is El Negro Felipe, and I am the son of the famous Liberator of the Slaves, El Negro Miguel, and I am working, as he did, for the absolute emancipation and freedom for people like us from people like you. And if you hang around long enough, I'll teach you some great songs about that. *(He smiles)* You have a tambor? I can make all these guys happy before they have to go off to your mine tomorrow, to sweat and haul rocks that make you rich.

Captain Alonzo: Ok ok… enough, Tapia. Take this idiot outside . . .

Bartolome: In the name of God Captain, we'll take over now.

Nectorio: We have some drums you can use left over from our last Encomienda.

Nectorio pulls out 2 primitive drums made out of logs, and a percussive piece of bamboo, called a "tiki-tiki", as is common in Barlovento with the Africans— El Negro and his boys get right on it. They organize the vocal and instrumental parts of an Afro-Venezuelan tambor song.

Juan del Prado de la Talavera *(the Encomendero of the Mission) and his daughter **Ana Carolina** enter. Ana seems distant and somewhat lost, as she has given up her child to be raised in the new world. The friars go to greet Sr. Prado humbly, for their existence depends on him.*

Bartholeme: How are you Señor Juan Encomendro del Prado de la Talavera? We were not expecting you until tomorrow.

Juan: Just checking on the new crew. How are things going here Nectorio? Everybody getting along?

Nectorio: As well as can be expected on the first day Sir.

Bartholeme: We have a gentleman here by the name of Negro Felipe who is about to entertain us with some music. *(He smiles)*

Ana Carolina: Oh Papa, we are just in time!!

Her mood has shifted when she sees the drums.

Juan: We cannot stay, my darling— tomorrow is a workday. Which is why I came . . . Nectorio, how many of them will be ready to work tomorrow?

Nectorio: All but one sir.

Captain Alonzo: Not to worry about this savage Chief Tamanaco. He will be at the mine by dawn with everybody else.

Bartholeme: *(quickly changing the subject)* Are we ready for the music?

El Negro: Listo y allegre…. Vamos! *The drumming begins.*

    LA NEGRA TOMASA (Traditional African/Venezuelan tambor)

> **Estoy tan enamorado de la Negra Tomasa**
> **que cuando se va de casa— que triste me pongo**
> (I am so in love with the Negra Tomasa, that when she leaves
> the house, it makes me so sad)
> **Lo mas' que me gusta la café, que ella me prepara**
> **Lo mas' que me gusta la comida, que ella cocina"**
> (I like the coffee she makes me— I like the food she cooks for me.)[48]

During this display, both the Natives and the Africans begin to dance. Even Ana Carolina gets carried away by the repetition and the beat. She is almost ecstatic, when suddenly….

Ana Carolina: Papa look!!!!! *She points to the statue of Mary, weeping blood. The music stops. Everybody becomes frozen and speechless, staring at Mary.*

Bartholeme: Holy Mother, Queen of Heaven, what is happening?

The Natives begin to sniff and describe the smell of sweet fragrant roses. Only Ana can understand the words of the Virgin now. Ana Carolina slowly tries to speak as she fixates on the Virgin's face and repeats the Virgin's words verbatim.

Ana: She weeps blood for the pain caused by the ball and chain (*Thorn of Crowns*) which sabotages and takes away the power and the strength of the Third World Man.

Nectorio: *On his knees crossing himself, he is clearly moved by the events, ignoring what Ana says.*

> **"O kindly mother of the redeemer,**
> **you who are still the open gate of**
> **heaven and the star of the sea;**
> **aid this fallen people which strives to rise;**
> **You who gave birth to your holy father,**
> **while Nature looked on in wonder."**
> *Advent antiphon Alma Redemptoris mater"*[49]

Mary: *(Heard only by Ana Carolina)* Here my child, the Universe brings you to see with your own eyes the beauty of these indigenous people, and how much they need a Queen to protect and unite them. Your daughter, Maria, will someday be this, Queen.

Ana Carolina: Oh, tell me mi Reina, how is my precious baby Maria? How I long for her.

Mary: Maria is under great care and love of her native Grandmother and La Negra Hamurapi.

Ana: It has been 15 years, Madre, I miss her so much.

Mary: You have made a humanitarian sacrifice for a larger cause dear Ana. With my power, Maria will triumph with the compassion of a holy mother, over the tyranny of these controlling Imperialists.

Ana: But she is lost in the jungle... so far away from me. *She breaks down.*

Mary: Weep not. She is surrounded by the love of nature and will come to represent the Holy trinity of the three races. Do not cry. You make me cry. I know your pain. I lost my son, but he still exists in spirit, as I do… and he gave his life for humanity.

Ana: I want so much to see her. But she will not leave her sanctuary.

Mary: Maria is beautiful and is becoming a beautiful young woman. Pray for her…

Ana: Yes, I remember when you told me I would carry a saint… when we were in Spain. And yet, I have been so confused about her welfare.

Mary: She is destined for God's work.

Ana: I am so sorry that I made you cry Santa Madre.

Mary: My heart bleeds for so many my child. I am glad you understand. All mothers make sacrifices for their children. So now… I have a job to do. Please tell these poor abused souls that I love them, and bless them all, and that I feel their suffering. I will bless them and take away their pain one by one. Please continue to pray the rosary every day and be strong.

Ana Carolina: Yes, mi Reina, I promise to be strong. *Ana wipes her tears and turns to address the slaves.*

The Holy Queen Mother told me to tell all of you that she loves you, and blesses you, and feels all of your suffering— And that the meek shall inherit the Earth. She will see you now.

Mary: Well, done my dear.

Ana Carolina: Thank you, Holy Mother. Now would it be possible for the others to be healed? They are in such pain.

Mary: Yes of course, ask Brother Bartholeme to play my song. Let's see if they accept my blessing.

Ana whispers to Bartholeme, who starts to play his mandolin, and a magical blaze of light appears in front of the statue of the Virgin. Everyone is spellbound as Mary's voice fills the air along with the smell of roses.

MARY SONG— DE INNOCENTIBUS— **To the Innocents**

> **"Our King is eagerly ready**
> **to welcome the blood-witness of the Innocents.**
> **Angels gather in chorus singing highest praise**
> **yet the clouds cry out in pain over the Innocents' blood.**
> **Glory be to the Father, the Son and Holy Spirit.**
> **And the clouds cry out in pain over the Innocent's blood."**

Hildegard of Bingen

Scene 4 — Carrying the Cross
— Tamanaco's Gladiator Death

Capitan Pedro Alonzo struts onto a dark barren stage holding a torch.

Pedro Alonzo: In the name of the Crown of Spain and the Holy Roman Catholic Church, I sentence you, Cacique Tamanaco to death, for innumerable crimes committed against her Majesty's people. We have planned a rather special execution to offer a, shall we say— diversion for your people, by testing the level of your courage. Inside a caged amphitheater you will fight in single combat, a war dog of singular bravery named Amigo. If you can defeat this beast, then you will be offered liberty and your life.

Tamanaco: I accept!

He stands in the circle waiting for the dog to be released on him, praying that his strong arm will bring a quick triumph. Seeing the animal come out to attack him, Tamanaco screams in Mariche language.

Tamanaco: "Today you will die at my hands, and Spaniards will learn that there is no danger in the world that can make a coward of Tamanaco."[50]

The dog, Amigo, turned on him with extreme ferocity, pawing at his chest, threw him to the ground within moments. There, the bloodstained dog rips Tamanaco's head from his body, using his claws. Mary walks on stage and kneels down near the bloody body of Tamanaco.

Mary: News of this gory spectacle, which caused horror even among those who had conceived it, spread quickly among the tribes. In order to avoid a similar fate, Natives pledged obedience to Pedro Alonso and the Crown. And, the rebellion of the Mariches, the most obstinate tribe of the great Cacique of Venezuela— Tamanaco, was thus suppressed. Here lies a beautiful man, who wanted only to protect his people and to live in peace on the Earth the creator gave him. May his brave soul rest in peace.

Scene 5— The Crucifixion
— The Transformation—

Mary remains in her pool of blood holding what's left of Tamanaco's body together. She wraps his body in her robe and sings AVE MARIA again. Tamanaco's two children, La India Tivisay, and his son, Terapaima, carry him to the water where the water goddess Yara waits for him, and takes him back into her arms.

Yara: "My altars are the mountains and the ocean, Earth, air, stars, all that springs from the great Whole, who hath produced, and will receive the soul." George Byron[51]

There is music and a sudden flight of butterflies over the water (Maria Lionza personally told me that whenever I see a butterfly, to know that she is visiting me.) This fluttering sound is followed by the beat of a hoofed, galloping animal, mixed with the sounds of forest animals. Slowly we hear the vocal strains of Ave Maria, this time sung by Maria Lionza (age 16) who enters naked and singing at the top of her lungs, astride her tapir (see photo), holding the bone of a female pelvis high above her head.

Maria de la Onza: I am Maria de la Onza, Maria de Leonza, Maria Lionza . . . I come to deliver and bless this beautiful soul, el gran Cacique Tamanaco. His courageous sacrifice made in the name of saving his people, has not been in vain. I am the incarnation of the Virgin Maria and Yara, Pre-Colombian Goddess of the Waters. Ponce de Leon chose to name me Maria de la Onza del Prado de la Talavera de la Reina de la Coruna, after my royal Spanish blood. I ride on the back of an onza, and from that I get my true name. Sometimes they think I am the Virgin of Coromoto. My mother was a Spanish immigrant, and my father was a native Caquetio who became Count William Guare de la Coruna and suffered much pain trying to live between both the worlds of the white man and his native people. I cannot split myself like that, so I have chosen my place in nature, on the mountain of Sortes in Chivicoa, Yaracuy. My mission is to unite the races by living harmoniously, to bring love and peace into the world, and to forbid all types of murder of animals, plants, or humans on my land.

I am the champion of the poor and the sick, and the disenfranchised. My mission is to enable people to fulfill their positive destinies, no matter how little they possess in this world—To correct disease through the forces and remedial plants of nature— and to accelerate the evolution of devoted souls towards enlightenment. I believe in God the Father, the Son and the Holy Ghost and they are my direct link to the divine along with all of the nature spirits of Mother Earth's sacred paradise. I have chosen to live my life as a hermit, deep within the jungle where I am protected by the Earth's creatures. I offer refuge to all pilgrims of any faith in my natural sanctuary, where they can come to be healed, or to be safe from the attack of malevolent forces.

I am, and always will be a Virgin, in a land where strong native men and women were raped, conquered and plagued by the white man's disease, along with African slaves who were also exploited. My people are in a state of modernity shock. They carry the blood of three races in a world that is still dominated by white Western culture. I now work with the great Chief Guaicaipuro and the Negro Felipe in an effort to make right these wrongs.

She continues: It is not Catholicism and the Church that the frustrated male and the disenfranchised, virgin female[52] are calling out to - It is me, their Queen Maria Lionza ... I will relieve their pain. Come to my mountain and you will witness miracles never touched by the western world.

END ACT II

INTRODUCTION – ACT III

THE MYSTERIES OF MARIA LIONZA

Act III will take you through the Glorious Mysteries of the rosary to Maria Lionza's present day practice on the Mountain of Sortes, six hours east of Caracas in Chivicoa, Venezuela. Every Friday night pilgrims from all parts of Venezuela pile into buses and make the long weekend journey to this mountain to redeem their souls, find cures, determine criminals, get romantic advice, have healthy babies, have businesses blessed, and much more. Maria Lionza is the key to all of this in Venezuela, and after making the sign of the traditional Catholic cross, one must pray to her for tangible results.

In Act I, I established that Maria del Prado de la Talavera de la Reina was an actual living person (with a Spanish mother and Venezuelan Indian father) whose destiny brought her as a child to the feet of the Virgin Mary in apparition.

I now believe that some of the Virgins are really 'Mary' in all her different characters. Others were actual living holy women (like Maria Lionza), whose missions were to serve humanity in the flesh and spirit through the archetypal role model of the Virgin Mary. Some were beatified, and others remained, like the Black Madonnas, as part of the subaltern religion and mythology. The validity of thousands of apparitions of the Virgin Mary, in all her manifestations has not been confirmed by the Catholic church. This Maria is very real and truly accessible through the practice of "spiritism."

Maria Lionza is unique in that the church does not accept her revolutionary racial Trinity of the Three Powers (with the Negro Felipe and the Indian Chief Guacaipuro). This was born of the Native and African population after the Spanish Conquista and colonization in the 1500s. Despite the continued use of Catholic prayers and beliefs, the Cult of Maria Lionza is still ignored by the Catholic Venezuelan Church. However, you will see how her devotees still go to Mass as part of the practice.

The shamanic practices, prayers, and rituals included in this dramatic text are revealed exactly as I witnessed them over a period of three years while living in Venezuela and practicing with these priests and priestesses of Maria Lionza. The characters, Marion and Manuel, are two real mediums who taught me much of what I know and introduced me to a huge pantheon of spirits. Many of the scenes depicting spirit are true to my experience, including the scenes with Simon Bolivar, Tamanaco, and Dr. Jose Gregorio. (In fact, the late Hugo Chavez, who was commander of the Fuerzas Armadas, and a devotee of Maria Lionza's cult, became Venezuela's President as a result of a revolution I witnessed in 1992.)

Maria Lionza embodies the same qualities of love and compassion as the Virgin Mary and provides one more important blessing. One can actually talk to her and many of her holy helpers to get spiritual, medical, financial, or romantic support and counsel in times of crisis. She descends rarely, and usually in only the bodies of mediums of high light.

And although I am not a medium. there is no doubt that she is using me to speak as I write this manuscript, for it has poured out of me. I am honored that she actually crowned me in 1992 and christened me as her God child in a special ceremony before I left the country. I hope that my eyewitness experience is properly conveyed to you through the magic of this musical-drama format.

Most of the songs and the prophet's poetry I have transcribed and translated from a cassette tape that I bought at a Perfumeria in Chivicoa. In the archaeo-mythologist, Maria Gimbutas's research tradition, I've assimilated so much about Maria Lionza's connection to Yara, the pre- Colombian water goddess mermaid. From the poetry and songs on this tape, one can understand her beloved protection over nature's flora and fauna, and most of all the passionate devotion she inspires in thousands of her followers. The street paperbacks of prayers and oraciones have also been handy, including a plethora of spell books in the witchcraft tradition ("brujeria"), with recipes for special banos (baths), despojos (aura cleaner/ exorcizers), trabajos (magical artworks), and candle art.

I am grateful for the opportunity to be able to share this experience in the context of my studies with Charlene Spretnak and her investigation of "Mary, Queen of the West". I hope that the anthropological aspects of my research have been suitably presented in this artistic form to enhance the mystical and spiritual profoundness of my experience. Although this property would be better rendered on film, I can still imagine how I would mount it on stage. Depending on the feedback I get from producers to whom I plan to submit this play, I can imagine mounting it as a bi- lingual production for Latin American audiences to celebrate its rich existing cultural magic. My dream, of course, has always been to mount my work on Broadway. Always lighting candles…...

I hope you enjoy the work,

    Cecilia Diaz Gruessing
12/1/99   San Francisco

ACT III—

THE GLORIOUS MYSTERIES

Characters

- **Maria Lionza**— herself— half white/half native, long black hair, beautiful green eyes
- **Negro Felipe**— African man, dressed as a soldier, with stutter
- **Guaicaipuro**— Indian Chief— 40s
- **10 humble street people**— Catia barrio, Caracas
- **Poet/Prophet**— 50-year-old man
- **Marion**— 38-year-old indian woman, nurse, bruja, medium
- **Sophia**— 20-year-old daughter of Marion— also medium
- **Luis**— 22-year-old boyfriend of Sophia, drummer
- **Luz**— 8-year-old daughter of Sophia, granddaughter of Marion
- **Rafael**— 28-year-old boyfriend of Marion, drummer, medium

Clients:

- **Cero**— Afro-Latino man— 50s
- **Martin**— Cero's 20-year-old, alcoholic son, Afro-Latino
- **Hugo Chavez**— Military commander turned revolutionary— 35 ish
- **Cecilia**— gringa tourist 34— American blond
- **Rosita**— young pregnant Afro-Caribbean lady— 23
- **Veruska**— 25-year-old white beauty— Miss Venezuela
- **6 other clients:** Prophet, 2 drummers, musician, 2 women
- **Manuel**— thin white man, medium— 30
- **Ana Gonzalez**— 40-year-old woman patient
- **Jazmin** (played by Cecilia)— assistant of Maria Lionza
- **Yarita** (played by Veruska) - assistant of Maria Lionza

Scene l— The Resurrection— Semana Santa & Easter Sunday — Catia, Caracas, Venezuela, April 1995

Scene 1— Calle del Barrio (Ghetto street)

The lights come up on the teeming market life of a Caracas urban street barrio, Catia, on Easter Sunday. The opening choreography presents a hybrid population, mixed with the Native Venezuelan Indigenous people, the African slave descendants, some Trinidadian (East Indian) influence, and the Criolle Caucasian Spanish. A backdrop-screen portrays a "perfumeria" with hanging herbs, religious regalia, and a sign saying "Perfumeria Las Tres Potencias" with the image of El Negro Felipe, the Holy Queen Maria Lionza, and El Cacique Guaicaipuro suspended over a Venezuelan flag. Standing in front of the store is a life size statue of Maria Lionza astride her danta. The store is flanked by a food market on one side, and a fabric store on the other. Above the Perfumeria, is a second-floor balcony one can reach by a downstairs doorway saying "Consultos Espirituales." It is ll am in the morning and the streets are lined with merchants selling everything from "hallacas" (Venezuelan holiday tamales) to last minute Easter regalia. Churchgoers are wearing their purple cotton robes over their ghetto best. The sound of salsa mixed with the street noise has provided the music for this stylized opening number. The mood switches with the distant sound of a slow, brass church band.

An eccentric street poet/prophet sits next to the statue of Maria preaching and singing to the church band back-up, with great urgency and drama:

Poet/prophet:

> "The city is lost ….
> And the anguished people run wild on the highways and the streets,
> Desperately … not knowing which way they are supposed to go …
> The crops don't matter,
> the human being driving at your side doesn't matter
> What's important is speed, and that there is triumph.
> The pedestrian is no longer important

timidly waiting for a light that never will change
The accident of a possible friend doesn't matter-
-- Nor the hand of a beggar,
Nor the ball of a little boy,
Nor the smile of the flower girl,
Nor, well ...... nor love.

A big car passes ......

a small car passes the statue on the wide highway

Where she is seated on a danta,

nude to the sun, strong, firm and erect,

Mounted over the city, like a symbol of love,

She is nailed into the earth of her ancestors,

the real owners of this land...

those who were dispossessed of their homes, of their truth, of their culture ...

Maria Lionza is there—
in the middle of this terrible culture where love and the
truth don't mean anything
Maybe that's why she is there, rising up
from the virgin earth with a woman's pelvis in her hand ...
Indian Goddess, like a wakeup call,
to remind us of our actual birth and ancestry."

(transcribed and translated from cassette tape)

A procession of Catholic church officers and purple clad congregation members slowly parades down the street, carrying three separate images of Jesus Christ and his Holy Mother: The first is Jesus wearing the crown of thorns, and his purple cloak, carrying the cross with Mary following; the second, is Jesus on the Cross with Mary at his feet; the third is Mary holding the dying Jesus in her lap (like the Pieta). The brass and percussion band is out of tune, playing a slow dirge to which people march in solemn procession en route to the Cathedral in the plaza, where Easter Mass will take place.

Scene 2— Inside the Centro de Las Tres Potencias
— (The Center of the Three Powers)

As soon as the parade passes, the street begins to change shape, the balcony over the Perfumeria empties, the backdrop lifts, and we go inside to Marion's mysterious sanctuary of magic, dominated by her multi-dimensional altar of spirits and animas where she will receive clients for spiritual consultations during this highest holy day of the year, Easter and the resurrection.

Marion's Altar

Marion's indoor/outdoor city apartment serves as her spiritual center (centro), her home, and as a menagerie for her pet birds, snakes, chickens, and dogs. She is a registered nurse and grandmother in her early fifties with her daughter Sophia, son-in-law Luis, granddaughter Luz, and young drummer lover, Rafael. She puts on some music as they transform from church attire to their "spiritual work clothes." They quickly wash down the altar and the busts. All three of these young people have been trained as mediums and bancos (assistants) and know the routine. Marion counts her cash from the altar, consults her list, and gets ready to send her team out on errands to buy altar paraphernalia and food.

> **Marion:** Pues....... Gracias a Dios that we went to the early Mass; we are expecting so many clients today, I'm a little backed up. SO, I've got the cash. We need: flores amarillos, incensio, candles, frutas, arroz, yucca (yam)/, and liquores— and fast because when this Mass lets out, we are going to have a line around the block with this full moon— Madre Gracias!

Marion looks up at the altar, crosses herself. Handing out cash as she designates buyers, she informs the group . . .

> **Marion:** Luz stays with me so we can clean up both physically and spiritually— the oldest and the youngest, right mi muchachita?
> *Little seven-year-old Luz jumps into her arms with enthusiasm.*
>
> **Rafael—** Marion, what kind of liquor?
>
> **Marion:** Let's see ...... Rum for Negro Felipe, Cocuy for our people, Anise for the Malandros, Aquardiente for the corte Africano . . ..
> what else?
>
> **Sophia:** Red wine of course for la Reina!
>
> **Marion:** Of course! How could I forget? And we need Holy water too, Ok? Please hurry...You can get most of it downstairs.

They all leave except little Luz, who begins to sweep, and clean the area while Marion washes down the altar and statues with a special concoction of ammonia, water, lemon, flowers, and special essencias. She talks to the statues as she tenderly washes them. She knows that the Negro Felipe does not like water, so he must be carefully dusted. She prays and conjures a cigar. Christ on the cross hangs high over the altar, with the next highest level being devoted to Maria, Felipe, and Guaicaipuro. The altar is eclectic and international including, Catholic Saints, Indians, Africans, Asians, leaders, doctors, and religious deities, known and unknown from all corners of the Earth. Marion crosses herself with a cigar.

> **Marion:** En el nombre de Dios Poderoso, el hijo, y el espiritu santo, yo pido permiso a mi Santa Reina Maria Lionza, el Libertador, el Negro Felipe, y el Gran C acique Indijeno Guaicaipuro, para conjurar este puro (tabaco), con intenciones de trabajar hoy, dia, sagrada de la Semana Santa— Pedir permiso de todos los Santos, espiritus, y animas que viven cercita, para darnos proteccion, amor, paz, evolucion, sabiduria, abundancia, y salud en nuestra viaje de la vida. Gracias, Amen.
>
> (In the name of God the Father, the Son, and the Holy Ghost, I Marion de la Luz, ask permission to my Holy Queen Maria Lionza, to the great liberator of the slaves, El Negro Felipe, and to the mighty Indian chief Guaicaipuro, to conjur this cigar, with intentions of working here today, this sacred day of Holy Week. I ask permission of all the Saints, spirits, and animals that live near, to give us protection, love, peace, evolution, knowledge, abundance, and health in our journey through life. Gracias and Amen)

After making the sign of the cross again, Marion lights the cigar and puffs smoke towards the four cardinal directions, observing the direction of the smoke and the designs of the cigar ashes. This is how Marion will determine if the spirits give her permission to work. She puffs away at the cigar as she begins to recite a special prayer to Maria Lionza, snapping her fingers throughout the oracion in the sign of the cross around the cigar smoke.

> **Marion:** In the name of God Almighty, I, Marion de la Luz ask permission to work in this hour and in this moment, to smoke this tobacco for the protection and help of all Sentient beings who come to this altar today.
> In the name of all the spiritual courts represented at this sacred altar,
> I ask your support and guidance on this holy day: I call Maria Lionza, all the saints of the Celestial Court and all of her "Don Juan" divas of the rivers, mountains, flora and fauna. I call all the great Caciques of the Venezuelan Indian Resistance; The political Pantheon of Simon Bolivar; The Seven African Powers of the Yoruba, Santeria cult; The

medical court of Dr. Jose Gregorio Hernanadez, Doctor of the poor. the ferocious court of the Vikings; the great North American Indian Chiefs; the court of the "malandros" (dead, repentant criminals); the great Buddhas, the Hindu deities, the Egyptian Kings and Queens, ancestors and angels. I ask you all to descend upon these innocent souls today with love, compassion, integrity, and healing wisdom. Amen que se sea.

(This geographical vortex seems to be unlimited in its ability to receive energy from different, epochs, nationalities, and life forms.)

Marion makes the sign of the cross with the smoked cigar, tosses it and Luz runs to study the position in which it fell on the floor, for this sign determines the absolute yes or no for the session.

Luz: Esta bien Abuela?

Marion: Yes, gracias, Reina. You see, Luz, how the cigar points straight at her. It's a GO, come on, let's make it beautiful!

The rest of the team returns, and goes to work fixing up the altar with fresh flowers, offerings of fruits, cake, cigars, liquor, special protection necklaces, etc. The bust of Maria Lionza is given fresh makeup and perfume. A big blue candle is lit in front of her, yellow for Guaicaipuro, red for Negro Felipe. (These are Venezuela's flag colors, representing the races.) The altar is being prepared as a "portal" to be crossed by spirits into our world.

Marion's young lover, Rafael begins to bang on the tambor, and the candles flicker madly as Marion prays to the sound of the drum.

"Oh, Milagrosa Reina Maria Lionza,	*Oh Miracle Queen, Maria Lionza*
Virgin que sacrificaste tu esplendorosa belleza	*Virgin, sacrificing your splendorous beauty*

en aras del amor a Cristo	in altars of love to Christ
a cambio te concedio el don infinito	who in exchange gave you the infinite gift to heal, to endure, to assist, to intercede,
de remediar, durar, socorrer, abogar	
y consolar a tus semejantes en este mundo terrenal Pidote de rodillas y con infinita devocion	& to console your people in this world I ask you on my knees with infinite devotion
me concedas lo que aqui humildemente te ruego si es para bien y gloria vuestra.	to grant me that which I humbly ask you in the name of your glorious goodness,
Amen	Amen.
Maria Lionza, belleza infinita, hacedme bendita. Tu culto es la gloria, tu nombre es Maria	Maria Lionza, infinite beauty, make me blessed...Your cult is glorious, your name is Maria
Concedenos todo, en este gran dia..."	Grant us everything in this great day.

Pilgrim: "Tu amor es la antorcha que alumbra el camino de vuestra conciencia. Bendigame con tu luz de fe, de esperanza."

Translation (Your love is the anchor that illuminates the road of our consciousness. Bless me with your light, your faith and your hope.)

Pilgrim: "Reina Maria Lionza, por tu poder, por los Siete Potencias que te acompanan, no dejes que las estrellas me maldigan, no que el Cielo me borre la ilusion, ni que Satanas ni los brujos me destruyan este pobre corazon."

Translation (Queen Maria Lionza, for your power, for the Seven Powers that accompany you, don't let the stars malign me, don't let heaven erase my illusion, nor Satan, nor the Brujos destroy this poor heart[1].)

The devotees, clients and more drummers are arriving with the call of the drum.

The Mysteries of Maria Lionza

Clients: Cero, an older Black man, 56 years old

Hugo Chavez, a Venezuelan Army commander, 42

Cecilia, a Gringa tourist, 35

Rosita, a young pregnant Afro/Latina woman, 19

Veruska, an exotic Miss Venezuela contestant, 25

More drummers arrive. Marion greets everyone and asks them to make their offerings in front of the altar as she brushes them with branches of rue, to distance any negative energy. She purifies them with the smoke of her conjured tobaccos. The bancos also help fumigate (smudge with tobacco) a line-up of clients who lift their palms and gaze mystically into the altar, swaying to the intoxicating beat of the drum, the repetition of the song, and the rhythm and "fuerza" (strength/ spiritual energy) in the room. They have all come from confession, Easter Mass & Communion, and are ready for some magic. Marion soon falls into an effortless transport, and without question, the first arrival is of Maria Lionza. The bancos prepare Maria Lionza's blue cape, her rose, crown and scepter, and a beautiful goblet of red wine. The drumming stops, and the crowd is silent as **she sings the Ave Maria**. *The real Maria Lionza is on the theatrical catwalk above.*

Maria Lionza (Marion as): *(after singing and getting dressed)* Maria Lionza les bendice a todos en el nombre de Dios, Jesus Christo, y el espiritu Santo. (ML blesses everyone in the name of God, Jesus, and the Holy Spirit.)

Rafael, Son in Law: Buenas Tardes Reina Madre. Bienvenido a su casa, y a nuestro centro humilde en el nombre de usted y Las Tres Potencias— con el Negro Felipe, y el gran cacique Guacaipuro.

(Good afternoon, Queen Mother, welcome to your home, and our humble center in your name and the name of the Three Powers, with the Negro Felipe and the Great Chief Guaicaipuro)

Maria: Gracias, Me alegre estar aqui contigos para celebrar la resurecion de Jesus Cristo. Y como hay mucho gente a servir hoy, te digo con todo mi corazon que estoy aqui para solucionar todas sus problemas con mi gran equipe de espiritus trabajadores de Dios, llena de fe y amor para ustedes.

(Thank you, I am happy to be here with you to celebrate the resurrection of Jesus Christ. And as there are many people to serve today, I tell you with all of my heart, that I am here to resolve all your problems with my great team of God's spiritual workers, who have much faith and love for all of you.)

A. SCENE WITH CERO

She begins to walk around the patients and blesses each one of them with a handshake that makes the sign of the cross. Approaching Cero, a middle-aged Black man

Maria (Marion): Dios, te bendice Señor .... Don't be nervous Señor Cero .... I'm here to help you.

Cero: Thank you, Reina. I am honored and grateful to be in your presence.

Maria: It's your son. I understand that he has a drinking problem.

Cero: Yes, Madre, and we are desperate, for he is gone again.

Maria: Tranquila mi hijo... he will be back. We know that with the invention of alcohol have come many good times, and also much disease of addiction. There is a remedy however, which will end his desire once and for all. You must bring him to my mountain to bathe in the holy waters of the river Yaracuy. Bring me 33 white candles and obtain the urine of a very old giant macho turtle, which when mixed in his food will cause him to lose all desire for alcohol. Guaicaipuro taught me this, and it worked for many victims of the bottle. I want your son to be healthy.

Cero: Thank you and God Bless you, Reina— you don't know how much grief he has brought to the family.

Maria: He is not a bad man. He is in pain. The alcohol shoots holes in his system and other negative energies and entities enter and dominate his weak ambition dictating his actions. If he is willing to be helped, we can do a "despojo" in one spiritual session. You must all pray the rosary and let him hear you. God bless you Cero, for trying to help your dear son.

Cero: Gracias Señora, my family is my life.

B. SCENE WITH THE GRINGA

Maria (Marion as): And now the Gringa, whom I have been watching. I have many things to say about your countrymen, but that is for another time mi hija. What can I do for you now?

Gringa: Excuse me mam, but I feel like I am dreaming. Could I be in an alternate reality?

Maria: No, of course not, I'm really here and so are you, everybody else, and all the spirits…. We are all God's children. Why would you doubt that?

Gringa: Well, this is all like the movies for me. An inexplicable miracle has brought me to your feet, even though I thought you were merely a legend. But my scholastic inquiry sees that you are absolutely here talking to me!

Maria: And now you know that I am very real indeed. Why do you suppose we are meeting?

Gringa: Well, I think it is because I just lost my father, Joseph Gruessing, to a long struggle with liver Cancer, after years of painful chemotherapy and operations. The doctors knew he was terminal, and still fried him with chemicals. And all through it, I knew he needed undiscovered herbal and spiritual healing, but there was no alternative. After he died, everything I did had no rational direction. The Universe just picked me up and brought me to you.

Maria: I'm truly sorry about your father. He was not ready to die, but he was very brave, and we are taking care of him. There is a cure for cancer in Venezuela, which you will have formally explained to you by Dr. Jose Gregorio Hernandez Rodriguez of our medical court. I can see your father now, and he is a very kind man, reaching out to you now, with so much love.

Gringa: Please tell him I love him, and I miss him so much. And that I thank him for everything he has done for me, and all his love and support. That I have never found a man as caring and thoughtful and intelligent as he was. I lost a hero.

Maria: Don't cry my child. He can hear you, and he is in the loving arms of Santa Lucia and the Virgin of Carmen. Gringa Cecilia listen. We want you to learn about our plants, our remedies. God has created so many sacred plants on this Earth, which are equipped with properties to combat the diseases of man. In spirit, we can see microscopically how these properties catalyze each other to eliminate many powerful viruses. Our 'mapurite'[2], a relative of your pokeweed, combined with some other plant and insect elements, can wipe out cancerous tumors and all trace of malignancy in the blood.

Gringa: Queen Maria ....Do you think I could learn enough about this plant to help someone heal without chemotherapy.

Maria: Absolutely . . . This is the whole idea sweet Gringa....... that we get helped and help others in the name of universal love. When you come to the mountain, I will introduce you to Dr. Jose Gregorio, and you will learn of the alternative, natural medicine of the tropics. He is a very special man, a great un beatified Saint.

Gringa: This is very important to me. Yes, I want to do everything, meet everybody, and go everywhere. Thank you very much for this opportunity. I can feel the chills all over my body.

Maria: Bless you my child, because so many are dying of this disease in your country, and this plant really works. You are a soul of alta luz, and your humanitarian destiny is grand. You will not be alone forever.
I promise to help you.

Gringa: Thank you so much Maria.

C. SCENE WITH HUGO CHAVEZ

Maria (Marion as): And here we have el Commandante Hugo Chavez Frias— what a pleasant surprise. I remember your grandfather, "Maisanta[3]," the last great warrior on horseback.

Chavez: And it is with his spirit that I come to you today mi Reina.

Maria: Tell me what's happening my son.

Chavez: My Queen thank you for indulging me. *(He bows and crosses himself)*

Maria: Tell me what is in your heart Hugo.

Chavez: "With an impotent vision I see before my eyes, that all the principals that have formed me, have been trampled by the corruption of my superiors, to whom I'm supposed to be subordinate, obedient, and loyal. But how can I be loyal to that which has not been loyal to my Patria? Or to the Bolivarian ideals that are the Democratic origin of our country and nationality?"[4] There is no water in the street, no telephones, no schoolteachers, no sanitation services . These are the symptoms of the incompetent authority which dominates Venezuela now.

Maria: We are all seeing this corruption, again, 300 years after the intense struggle of our liberator, Simon Bolivar who gave his life to free us from the continuing ignorance of European oppression. I am confused and troubled by the corruption and incompetence of your president, Carlos Andres Perez. It troubles me greatly along with the great Indian Chiefs and African Slaves who fought for the same independence before Simon Bolivar. I clearly admire and deeply sympathize with the compassion and bravery you have for Venezuela. However, I must defer these issues of revolution and violence to our great Libertador himself, as I cannot endorse violence of any kind. You must come to the mountain, and he will empower you to do what is right in the eyes of God and our country. Your path is righteous yet full of obstacles, but I can feel Simon begging me to speak to you about this coup.

Chavez: Can I not speak to him now, Maria?

Maria: The time is not right, you must assimilate more data towards your own potential, and he will be of more value to you upon your next meeting. Trust me Hugo . . . This is his territory. You know, both General Gomez in the 1920's and 30's used to come to me for advice, as well as the dictator Marcos Perez Jimenez, in the fifties, and I could never advise violence.

Chavez: Mi Reina, I am here to tell you that there will soon be a revolution, that will harm innocent citizens of this great country of mine, and I come to you for support, understanding, and spiritual counsel at this time.

Maria: First, I must tell you that your grandfather, Maisanta, is asking me to send you his strength and support at this very moment. You have dedicated yourself to a very dangerous and noble path, for which some day you will become the President of this great Republic. But you must gather your people with honest heart. I can see that you are serious about this Coup, but . . . . Clearly Hugo . . . you are not yet organized. We ask you to become crystal clear. Then our Liberator, Simon Bolivar will respond to your prayers. He waits for you at my mountain. I bless you Hugo Chavez Frias with all my heart.

Chavez: As you wish my Holy Queen, I respect this advice, for I know that this is as much a spiritual journey, as it is a political and military transformation for our country. This is my mission, and I need your help in whatever way you can give it. I embrace you with my love, mi Santa Madre.

Maria: And I thank you for the humble Venezolanos who so desperately need a leader.

D. SCENE WITH ROSITA

Maria (Marion as): Dios te bendice hermana. How many months pregnant, are you?

Rosita: Gracias Madre, tengo 5 meses, but I think there may be something wrong because I am bleeding so much. I am worried because this is my first baby, and I want so much for her to be healthy.

Maria: Your baby is a boy, and you must refrain from drinking coffee or any type of alcohol . . . Let me see *(she embraces Rosita's belly from behind)*

Rosita: I don't drink coffee or alcohol madre.

Maria: *(pause)* Then someone has struck you ....the father of this child has shown you violence. Why is this happening??

Rosita: Because he is poor and frustrated and does not want this baby.

Maria: This baby must live, and he will be beautiful and full of goodness. You need the work of la India Rosa.

Rosita: She is my protectress. *(She holds up her pink and red beaded India Rosa necklace)*

Maria: You too must come to our next pilgrimage to the mountain and my river, and there she will treat you. Your baby is fine, we must now strengthen your uterus. You will need to bring yucca (yam) for my "materia" (medium) to prepare a special syrup for you, 21 pink candles, and many yellow flowers. And you must leave this man and go to your mother. He does not deserve any paternal rights to this soul inside of you, crying for love and life. Give your baby the name of Jesus, and he will be protected under my power and the Holy Father's. I will arrange for the India Rosa to see you on the mountain. Rosita, corazon, I am here for you. Pray the rosary with your heart and soul.

Rosita: Si Señora, *(weeping)* Thank you for everything my Holy mother. Here is a rose from my garden.

Maria puts the rose in her hair.

E. SCENE WITH VERUSKA

Maria (Marion as): Maria te bendice....... Veruska, how are you? My how you've changed.

Veruska: I'm very well thank you Señora *(bowing humbly)*

Maria: And your mother?

Veruska: She asked me to give you this special apple cake, baked in your honor on Easter for your sacred resurrection.

Maria: Thank your mother for thinking of me. I'm very touched. Now what can I do for you, as we all bathe in the radiance of your incredible beauty?

Veruska: Thank you mi Reina . . . I still live in the barrio with my mother, although I have unfortunately not inherited her cooking abilities.

Maria: Oh, now that's too bad.

Veruska: However, I am being trained and groomed by a special agency in Caracas[5] who is preparing me to run for Miss Venezuela in 1997.

Maria: And perhaps Miss Universe next I predict. Veruska, you are a beautiful woman inside and out, and you will have all my blessings.

Veruska: Thank you Maria . . .

Maria: We all know that Venezuela makes Goddesses. Am I right? We have developed a particular sensuality and charm, inherited from our multi-racial, hybrid roots. And also, from our ancient South American mythology of beautiful water goddesses who use their dark exotic beauty, their light mystical eyes, their seductive voices, and their fish tails to hypnotize, fertilize, and make us want to love, with an urge to merge. We have "god mothers" of baseball teams; there are beauty queens in village holidays, of harvests, companies, and especially the Carnival Queens. Every last pueblo has an Immaculate Patron Saint. Even in prisons we crown beautiful, convicted women. Our matrilineal roots have created queens everywhere who inspire a liturgical respect. Tell me how are these beauty groomers cultivating your spirit my child?

Veruska: Maria, I cultivate my own spirit. And I have decided to advance my knowledge of the rainforests. I want to protect our country's natural resources, and to propose legislation to outlaw the murder of all animals, to promote national vegetarianism, to improve the sanitation system, to start recycling, and to develop an ecological consciousness with children in the public schools. I need your help, Maria. This will be my platform— my mission for my country.

Maria: Veruska, your beauty is exuberant like a tropical forest, but your inner beauty and spiritual compassion is what will really carry you. I advise you not to be too distracted by the romance of men. For this will inhibit your strength as a leader of people. Men's adoration of women's beauty and sexuality is paradoxical in Venezuela.[6] Many Latina women are underpaid, oppressed, single, uneducated, and battered. Therefore, you, with your Diva like beauty and spirituality, must become a role model which delicately balances the high role of Goddess, while elevating the value of oppressed Venezuelan women. This you must accomplish in tandem with your feminine approach to ecology, and the protection of our Mother Earth— It is the same thing my child. Do you see? We are all Goddesses.
... When you are ready for a spiritual baptism, I will develop your faculties as a medium— a destaparse para desarollarse, oiste? Next time ....

Veruska: *(clutching her heart)* Oh Mother, what would I do without you?

Scene 3 — The Ascension
— Pilgrimage to the Mountain of Sortes, Chivicoa
(40 days after the Resurrection) May 1995

Scene 3a— Street scene in front of Botanica

It is a Friday night, on the street in front of Marion's Centro in Catia, and the same drummers segue into a continuing rhythm session as they wait for the pilgrimage to begin. An old school bus is being loaded with duffle bags, kitchen gear, food, religious props and tools, musical instruments, blankets, and hammocks. The bus says "Centro Las Tres Potencias," with crude paintings of el Negro, Maria, and Guaicaipuro on the side. The five featured pilgrims, along with others, are ready for the journey. Musicians, children, teens, and seniors are present, to make this Holy, six-hour Pilgrimage from Caracas to the Mountain of Sortes in Chivicoa, Yaracuy. Marion is checking her list and trying to organize seating for the passengers. Her family/team has finally loaded everything. Her cousin, Manuel arrives.

Marion: Hola Manuel, how wonderful you could make it.
(She embraces him and ushers him into the loaded bus.) Everyone, I would like you to meet my cousin, Manuel, a medium of the highest light that Venezuela has to offer. Buen Viaje everyone. Vamonos a Sortes— Arriba!!!!!

Scene 3b— The Journey in the bus

The bus radio broadcasts the famous Ruben Blades and Willie Colon *recording of the hit salsa song, "Maria Lionza."*

"En la Montana de Sortes de Yaracuy	*In the Mountain of Sortes in Yaracuy*
en Venezuela . . . Vive una diosa,en la Montana de Sortes por Yaracuy . .	*in Venezuela . . . . A goddess lives in the Mountain of Sortes in Yaracuy*

Vive una diosa, una noble reina de gran belleza y de gran bondad Amada por la naturaleza, Illuminada de caridad.	*A goddess lives, a noble queen, of great beauty and great generosity . . . Loved by nature, illuminated by charity . . .*
Y sus paredes son encantamientos, y su techo hecho de tejas bellas	*And your walls are enchantments, and your ceiling made with beautiful tiles.*
la luna, sol, el cielo, y la montana son companeros	*the moon, sun, sky, and mountain are your friends*
El rio, quebrada, y flores son sus mensajeros.	*The river, hills, and flowers are your messengers*
O Salve Reina Maria Lionza— O Venezuela	*Oh, Sacred Queen Maria Lionza— O Venezuela*
Y va velando con su onza cuidando su tierra entera,	*You ride across your land on your onza, vigilant*
desde el Guarijo hasta Cumana de los Latinos	*from Guajira to Cumana Cuida el destino Caring for the destiny of the Latinos*
Vivir unidos sin Libertad	*To live united without liberty.*

CHORUS

Maria Lionza y sus milagritos un ramo flores te voy a llevar	*Maria Lionza, for your miracles a bouquet of flowers I will bring you.*

Un ramo de flores de rosas blancas por la pureza de tu bondad,	*white for the purity of your goodness*
Maria Lionza y sus milagritos	
un ramo flores te voy a llevar	
Por toda la gente hasta los serritos	
que hay en Caracas protegera.	

(transcribed and translated from cassette tape)

The six-hour bus ride southeast to Yaracuy becomes a full-blown musical salsa dance and sing-along number that reflects the Afro-Native spirit energy of a busload of hopeful and happy pilgrims, ready as ever for a mystical experience. The 'Ascension' is reflected in the evolution of their city behavior, all the way from Caracas to the foot of the mountain where a mystical presence definitely takes over. They know they are about to climb the mountain of Maria Lionza. It is 3 am in the 'madrugada'(dawn) when they arrive and disembark from their dream states to greet the "Altar Mayor."

Above the stage is a catwalk throne where the real Maria Lionza, the Negro Felipe, and Chief Guaicaipuro sit monitoring the rituals below like a control tower.

Scene 4 — The Mountain of Sortes — Chivicoa, Venezuela

4a. The Altar Mayor— (Main Altar)

This is an important stop before one cross the bridge over the Yaracuy River to enter the sacred grounds of the Mountain of Sortes, a national park 6 hours from Caracas, set aside for pilgrims by the government of Venezuela. The Altar Mayor consists of three major shrine "rooms" to Maria Lionza, her Trinity, the Court of the Indigenous natives, and Dr. Jose Gregorio.

These three-sided, open-air altars are charged with dancing candle flames and fragrant flowers, where people smoke their first tobacco to call spirit, and make their offerings, promises, and requests. Marion organizes her team to hold hands as she crosses herself and prays on behalf of the group.

Marion: In the name of God, the Father, the son, and the holy ghost .... I call upon Maria Lionza, el Negro Felipe, Guaicaipuro, and all her courts: the Indians, the Africans, the Doctors, the Don Juanes of Nature, and all Cosmic forces of the Universal Mother and Father. Penetrate into each of our living cells so that each instant your love will fill us with illumination, understanding and peace. We thank you for this new day, our daily bread, and for all our benefactors. We pray for the peace of the world, for each one of us here today. We pray for shoeless children, for the hunger of the entire world, for our senior citizens, for invalids, for the sick, for those full of egoism or hate, grudges or desperation, that a ray of your light enters them to believe in Universal love. We pray for those who have lost their faith, for those who have been persecuted by justice, for prisoners just or unjust. We pray for disoriented and corrupt youth. We ask that you bring our government to a level of democracy that honestly serves our people, to organize our schools, and give light to our professors and scientists, to elevate our social services, to protect and reform our institutions with knowledge and wisdom. We ask these blessings for all who guide humanity. Madre— help us pray for our enemies, protect them, inundate them with love. Dispel us of all bad thoughts, of all arrogance, of all pride, of all stinginess, violence, and impatience. Help us to be generous, humane, and permit our spirits to regenerate the beauty of nature. We pray for all our ancestors, brothers and sisters, and children in the flesh and in spirit. Give the mediums the strength and the protection to fulfill the needs of those with us now. Allow us to be touched by your generosity and healing powers as we enter your sacred land.[7]

Everybody finishes their personal prayers, and before they make their way across the bridge in the early morning darkness, Marion invokes Don Juan del Rio Yaracuy for permission to cross.

Marion: En el nombre de Dios, etc., con la bendicion de su Reina Maria Lionza, pedimos permiso para nosotros, pelegrinos humildes, para cruzar su rio sagrado, Señor Don Juan de las Aguas. Buscamos la pureza de su Rio Yaracuy para limpiarnos, curarnos, y accelerar nuestra evolucion espiritual. Por favor, bendigan nosotros con su poder y gracia, Señor Don Juan de las Aguas.
(In the name of God, etc., and with the blessings of your Queen Maria Lionza, we ask permission for us humble pilgrims to cross your sacred river, Don Juan of the Waters. We seek the purity of your river Yaracuy to clean us, cure us and to accelerate our spiritual evolution. Please bless us with your power and grace.)

Scene 4b— The Ascension of the Pilgrims

They begin to sing.

Caminante pelegrinos	**Walking Pilgrims**
"Encontrastes el camino de la pena y la verdad	*You found your way in pain and in truth*
No le temas, no le temas el destino que te espera	*Don't be frightened of the destiny waiting for you*
es de bondad 2X	*It is of goodness*
Este caminito verde que va subiendo hacia monte	*This green path that winds up the Mountain*
Este camino de Sortes que esta encima del cerro	*This path of Sortes above the hill*
Es el altar de la Diosa, de la Reina Caquetia	*Is the altar of the Goddess, the Caquetia queen,*
Patrona de las cosechas, de dulce nombre, Maria	*Patron of the crops, and of the sweet name, Maria*

The Mysteries of Maria Lionza

Llega la noche	*The night arrives*
la luna espera	*The moon waits*
las mariposas que van llegando	*The butterflies are arriving*
ensenando pelegrinos y caminitos de Sortes	*Showing the pilgrims the paths of Sortes*

Continuing with another song:

Por la Noche Fresca	*By the fresh (beautiful) evening*
y la luna clara	*and the clear moon,*
que juegan el rio	*the river plays*
y con el aroma de tus lindas flores llena del rocillo	*and with the aroma of your pretty dewy flowers*
Voy hacer el barco de cosas floridas para ti mi Reina	*I will make a boat of flowered things for you my Queen Goddess of the waters, of the fertile land*
duena de los rios 2X	*owner of the rivers . . . .*
Por los caminitos, la que va cruzando tus lares,	*By the paths, those who go crossing your Bridges*
Son las mariposas que vuelan en tus altares,	*The butterflies fly over your altars*
Yo reze mi canto cerca la agua hasta arriba	*I recite my song near the water all the way up*
que llega, que anda camino a las serranias . . ."	*the path of the hills that winds and arrives.*

(transcribed from cassette tape)

They begin the long climb up the mountain singing to call Maria and the spirits, passing the portals of other groups of pilgrims, whose flaming altars, and passionate songs and drumming chants illuminate the way. The ambiance is mysterious and dream-like. Patients are ritually laid out, encircled by candles (velados), in front of their elaborately dressed altar., Some sleep, others *sing, drum, and shout out "fuerza" to bring down the next spirit's performance.*

It is a veritable Disneyland of passion, mystery, magic, and initiation as the young and old backpack in the dark, up the narrow river path to the summit of the holy mountain where Maria Lionza's Palace of the Coronation[8], or "Escalera" (staircase) waits for them. In blue dream light they ascend to the rhythm of the drum, energized by the enlightenment that awaits them above.

Scene 4c— The Queen Mother's Altar on the mountain peak

Upon arriving at the Queen's royal summit portal, everyone drops their packs, and falls to them knees in front of the stone "palace" altar and prays.

Marion: (*requesting permission through a conjured Tabaco*):

"Oh, miraculous Queen Maria Lionza. You who have sacrificed your splendid beauty for the love of Christ, without taking advantage of the pleasures that you have over the earth…. The powers that Christ gave you…. the infinite power to cure the sick, to come to the help of the people, to speak for them and console her followers on Earth. I pray on my knees and with an infinite devotion that you bless us with permission to work in this your sacred sanctuary, for our good and for your glory. Amen."[9]

They begin to sing, and Marion continues to invoke spirit with her tobacco.

"En la Montana de Sorte, en Yaracuy	*On the moutain of Sortes in Yaracuy*
hay una Diosa encantada en la noche tropical, desconcertante	*there is an enchanting goddess in the disconcerting tropical night*
y hermosa sobre una danta cabalga	*and so beautiful mounted on her danta.*
Es Maria Lionza, la que cuida las Culturas…	*It is Maria Lionza, she who cares for the culture*
duena de los animales, de los arboles y el agua, los pajaros y los nidos, la que enlucera el camino,	*Matron of the animals, trees, and the waters, the birds and their nests, she who illuminates the road*

The Mysteries of Maria Lionza

la que afina las guitarras.	*She who tunes the guitars.*
Es Maria Lionza de cabellos negro, y ojos claros	*It is Maria Lionza with black hair, and clear eyes*
eres muy rica en tesoro y en gran amor que derramas/	*rich in treasure, and great love that she spills—*
Te traere un ramo de rosas y canto de la sabana	*I bring you roses, and song of the land*
si tu me haces un milagro	*if you will make me a miracle.*
En la montana de Sorte la divinidad del bosque	*In the mountain of Sorte, the divinity of the woods*
tiene su reno y morada, Maria Lionza, Maria Lionza	*has her reign and residence, ML, ML*
Diosa nuestra madre y reina	*Our Mother Goddess*
Queen la diosa Venezolana.	*Goddess of Venezuela*
Maria Lionza, a ti el Indio perseguido	*ML, for you the persecuted Indian*
buscando su libertad lucho con fe y te invocaba	*looking for liberty, fought with faith, & invoked you*
Nunca olvides a tu gente el pueblo de Venezuela	*Never forget your people, your village of Venezuela*
que con gran fervor te clama.	*Who cry out for you with great fervor.*
Maria Lionza tus hijos aun sufrimos	*ML, even though your children suffer*
te pedimos nuevas fuerzas para continuar luchando	*we ask you for renewed strength to continue the fight*
que tu patria un dia sea libre	*So that one day your country will be free*

y que tu suelo sagrado no lo pisoteen extranos."	*And that your sacred ground is not trampled by strangers anymore.*

By Cristobal Jimenez— Llanero composer[10]

As they sing, Marion examines the tabaco, presents it to the pilgrims triumphantly. The ashes are white and fluffy. She gives the 'go' signal, and the pilgrims begin to build the altar with statues of the spirits of many pantheons who work under the protection of Maria Lionza. Candles are lit, offerings are made, liquor is spritzed over the altar, tabacos are conjured, and everyone makes their way to the river to purge, purify, and bathe ("despojos")[11].

Scene 4d— River Purification

In the river Marion and her "bancos" (assistants) smoke conjured tabacos around all the initiates with prayer for purification. A single drummer keeps the magical beat, and the river purge turns into a sacred mystical purification ritual. Candles are lit on the river rocks. A special drink is passed around which causes people to vomit, and purge. They are given a piece of special blue soap to scrub down with, and then toss downstream over the left shoulder. The water is cool, pure, and invigorating, surrounded by the majesty of natural jungle life, complete with tropical flowers, monkeys and birds and the magical presence of Maria Lionza and her huge pantheon of spirit helpers. Specially prepared herbal "banos" are administered on the banks of the river. The initiates shiver with the frigid purity of the early morning baptism. Multicolored beaded protector necklaces, knotted prayer belts, stars and crosses (including the Cruz de Caravacas) are all purified in the bath and river water, as well as smudged.

— *On the catwalk above there is a conference amongst the Three Powers, and they agree to send Guaicaipuro down first. It is not long before Marion's cousin, Manuel falls into trance standing in the water. He begins to shout and spin his arms madly splashing water everywhere. It is indeed, the great warrior and Cacique, Guaicaipuro*

Marion: Bienvenido hermano, adelante!!!

Guaicaipuro: Buenas tardes mi gente!! Listo trabajar!! Take me to the altar . . . (Good afternoon my people! I am ready to work!)

Scene 5 — The Descent of the Spirit
— Tongues of Fire and the work of the Pentacostal Brujos (witchdoctors)—

4e— Maria's Altar

*We return to the Queen's land altar where 'arepas con huevos' (cornmeal eggburgers) are being cooked over a "fogata" (fire). As the lights come up, we also hear the mysterious sound of the cicadas (locusts)12 in the trees. Marion has put finishing touches on the altar. The pilgrims are seated in a semi- circle in front of the altar. The work paraphernalia is ready to go holy water, dozens of different color candles, bottles of rum, anise, aquardiente, red wine, flowers, cigars arranged in the form of a cross, various offerings— food, fruit, herbs, incense, perfumes, agua de colonia, Nazarene crosses, knifes, pins, pieces of iron and magnets, feathered headdresses for the Indians, ribbons, walking sticks, hats, skirts, dresses, earrings, scepters, capes, crowns. Guaicaipuro (Manuel) is marking the four corners with his knife. The bancos follow him. He walks like a prehistoric man with what we might think is an angry expression on his face. He (Guaicaipuro) draws designs with white baby powder on the earth to create a star formation in front of the altar for the next stage of the "mystery" called **Velaciones or Velados**. Nine people are directed by Guaicaipuro (Manuel) to lay down inside this design forming the spokes of a wheel with their bodies (heads in the center), while bancos and assistants surround their individual bodies with small, different colored candles. Guaicaipuro looks over all of this activity with great care and dignity. From the catwalk, Maria Lionza and el Negro watch ceremoniously. Guaicipuro (Manuel) is given a handful of tobaccos which he holds up high to conjure:*

Guaicaipuro: Fuerza de la tierra, el viento, el fuego, y la agua, con Dios Poderoso— Por favor que esta hoja de tabaco, mi hacha sagrada, reciba la luz magnetica necesaria para ver la verdad, conocer el mal y combatirlo.

(Strength of the earth, wind, fire, and water, with God Almighty— make this leaf of tobacco, my sacred tobacco, receive the magnetic light necessary to see the truth, to know evil, and to combat it.)

The assistants (bancos) begin to puff sacred tobacco smoke over the bodies of the "meditating" initiates. Things begin to happen, when several people begin to go into trance simultaneously. This will be portrayed as a musical holographic dream/drama of descending spirits. Keep in mind that the following vignettes will crisscross in a three-ring circus manner, where the dialogues are sequential, but the stage is teeming with multiple spiritual encounters.

Guaicaipuro: Buena noche todo. Guaicaipuro come here to help you move your future. We watch you, and we protect you from evil.

Guaicaipuro walks around the circle of bodies observing the initiates and his cigar— looking up, taking swigs of cocuy. He stops in front of a young mestizo (African-Latino).

5A. SCENE WITH GUACIPURO AND MARTIN

Guaicaipuro: You are Cero's son, Martin, and I come to take drinking devil out of you. *(Martin begins to tremble on the ground, and his father Cero approaches, with a coca cola bottle filled with a special elixir including the urine of a macho turtle. Guacaipuro goes through an advanced transmutiation)* En el nombre de Dios Poderoso, I call upon the Seven African Powers[13] to help me exorcise the demon that drives this man to the bottle— I call upon all great Venezuelan warriors to protect this man once we take away the dark parasite spirit who is sucking his blood.

Martin begins to shake like crazy and leave his body, and the bancos lift him into a standing position. He takes on the body language of a monster who speaks in tongues and confronts Guacaipuro who waltzes around him like an animal ready to fight. The wrestling match begins, and Guacaipuro soon has the possessed Martin straddled across his shoulders, spinning him around as he shouts a war cry. He drops Martin onto the ground, who then regains his own consciousness.

Guacaipuro: Bring me the jarabe (syrup)!

Martin opens his eyes and Guacaipuro takes him in his arms like a baby.

Martin: Where am I?

The Mysteries of Maria Lionza

Guaicaipuro: I am Guaicaipuro, and we have healed you. But there is one more thing. Repeat after me I promise to drink this jarabe in front of the altar of our Holy Father and Mother and all my African and Indian ancestorsand promise never to touch a drop of alcohol again in my life . . ..

Martin repeats the promises one by one and drinks the jarabe as all the disciples and initiates watch. It is clearly distasteful, and he tries to reject it, but Guaicaipuro is firm. They watch Martin go through an exorcistic madness for 10 minutes upon swallowing the jarabe. On the catwalk above, Maria Lionza rises with vigilant concern, and el Negro gets ready to descend.

Guaicaipuro: Good....... Now *(He picks up a bottle of whiskey, takes a swig and pours it into Martin's mouth)*.......... you will drink this!!!

Martin: Please, I can't!!! This is crazy!! What are you doing?

Cero: Martin, have faith in spirit!

He forces Martin to drink pure rum alcohol which makes him really sick and throw up—Guaicaipuro takes him in his arms again and looks him close in the eyes saying

Guacaipuro: You must feel the pain. Drink this now!!!! You will never drink again for the love of yourself and your family. You understand this and you will serve the Great Spirit.

Everybody: Amen que se sea!!! *(Cero is weeping with joy. Guaicaipuro returns to the catwalk and Manuel returns to his body.*

Cecilia Anne Gruessing, M.A.

5B. SCENE WITH ROSITA, NEGRO FELIPE, & INDIA ROSA

Meanwhile, El Negro Felipe has entered Marion's body, and he is working on Rosita's pregnancy, cutting up melons and papayas which he mashes all over her pregnant belly, activating the concoction with doses of rum, which he intermittently sips.

El Negro speaks with a special stutter which is often confused for singing, but probably comes from his rum habit.

Felipe (Marion as): Oh, mi hija! You are so young and so precious, and your boy will be fine and healthy. The India Rosa will be here soon to bless you and your baby, but I am here to "quitar la pava". (get rid of the bad)

Rosita: Oh, Gracias hermano. My mother thanks you, my father, my baby thanks you how can I repay you?

Felipe: Listen to me hija. The father of this baby has another woman who is driving him crazy, and she has sent brujeria to you. But your protector, la India Rosa, has been with you always. We will sweeten your spirit, and pacify all negativity, we will make your spirit beautiful, and I will personally liberate you from the chains of this unevolved boyfriend of yours.

Rosita is shocked and upset by this information. Negro Felipe puts his hand on Rosita's belly and prays. Upstairs on the catwalk, Maria Lionza 'makes a spiritual call.'

Maria Lionza (as herself): At this time, I call upon the India Rosa to descend and help this innocent creature and her baby in their moment of need. I ask this in the name of the father, the mother, and the holy ghost.

Felipe: En este momento, en el nombre de Dios, el hijo, y el espiritu santo, Yo, el Negro Felipe, pido de mi hermana la reina Maria Lionza para ayudarme quitar la pava de esta mujer innocente. Alejele del padre de este nino para que ella puede olvidarle y abrir sus caminos para el bienestar del nino y la familia. (In this moment, in the name of the father, the son and the holy ghost, I ask my sister, the queen Maria Lionza, to help me remove the darkness from this innocent woman. Distance her from this baby's father so that she can forget him and open her roads for the well-being of the child and the family)

Marion's daughter, Sophia, has gone into trance with la India Rosa and approaches Rosita and el Negro Felipe, who makes a final blessing over Rosita and puts her under the care of la India Rosa. (El Negro has a love affair in spirit with the India Rosa.) Sophia has taken on spirit.

India Rosa (Sophia): Estoy aqui mi hija. Todo esta bien. Maria Lionza sent me to reassure you of my vigilance.

Rosita: I just feel so much better to hear your voice. Thank you, Rosa. Please tell me about my baby.

India Rosa (Sophia): You must understand that your baby was traumatized when you were struck, and in order to make the birth easy, we must strengthen your uterus with the yucca (yam) elixir, which has been prepared for you.

Marion returns to her body from Negro Felipe and fetches the special syrup. Then the India Rosa blesses it.

India Rosa: Learn this special yam recipe and drink this often mi hija, and I promise you an easy delivery in September. As for the father and his girlfriend .you should be thankful. She is gaining a problem you are losing..... (*Pause*) Do you hear me, Rosita? Do you understand me????

Rosita: Yes India, I feel like a fool. Thank you for waking me up.

India Rosa: You are young, you are beautiful and intelligent, with a loving Mother. You have a good heart, and I will always be there to take care of you and your baby. Better me than some cheating cabron! I bless you and ask you to keep roses by your bed to remember me. Te bendigo hija mia.

5C. SCENE WITH HUGO CHAVEZ and SIMON BOLIVAR

Maria *(from the catwalk):* Yes Simon, we hear you, and by all means, your moment has come to speak to Hugo Chavez. He awaits you passionately, as he does the liberation of our country. I trust your counsel will be the best Venezuela can offer.

Manuel has transformed into Simon Bolivar who descends coughing, which indicates that his appearance reflects the end of his incarnation when he had tuberculosis. He is blindly searching for Hugo Chavez, and Marion comes to his aid.

Marion: Bienvenido Libertador, we are honored by your presence and beg your blessing.

Bolivar (Manuel as): Gracias hermana por ayudar me a tierra. (Thank you, sister, for grounding me.) I bless this company of Venezuelans with every drop of the blood I once possessed, when I tell you that your Patria is on the brink of major revolution. I have been called by my Queen, Maria Lionza for the Commandante of the Fuerzas Armadas, Señor Hugo Chavez, to discuss the matter. I can wait no longer to be in his company.

Chavez: Commandante Hugo Chavez Frias at your service

Sir! *(Shouting and rising from his lying position.)*

Bolivar: Where is he! Take me to him!!

They embrace and weep, as everyone gathers round. Chavez gathers himself and prays on bended knee to Simon Bolivar:

Chavez: "Oh Great Liberator, Simon Bolivar, who came to this land guided by Divine Light and the Great Power of God and Divine Providence with which you liberated five nations" …. I thank the Queen Mother Maria Lionza, for this opportunity to meet you at last.

Bolivar: The pleasure is mine indeed. Where can we talk?

Chavez: Oh padre, mio, where have you been? The country is lost with these selfish leaders. Maybe now there is hope for the people. I don't know where to begin . . . everything is so dirty, dark, greedy, and corrupt . . . No electricity, no water, the schools are always on strike. I'm sick from it.

Bolivar: *(coughing)* Listen to me! You must take care of yourself, for your strength and clarity will determine the success of this golpe (coup). The situation is more serious than you know. They are transferring public funds to Swiss banks through the President's cocaine mafia: your telephone system is about to take a major crash; garbage collection in Caracas is three weeks overdue; and the children are rioting in the schools. This is MY country they are screwing around with— MY people!!! And it must stop!!

Chavez: Gracias a Dios, I know now that I am not alone. I salute you Commandante. You renew my frustrated heart and soul.

Bolivar: Oh no........This is Venezuela we are talking about, were the Trinity of the races will always reign. I spent too many years fighting for this flag, for these people, to watch my country fall back into the hands of greedy, unorganized Castillian opportunists. You must take over the state house in Caracas, abduct Carlos Andres Perez, track the stolen funds, kick his mistress out of the country, announce a military takeover, and have a press conference. I will help you.

Chavez: That exact plan, minus the extrication of Carlos Andres' mistress, has been waiting only for your command sir, for I have studied your work, and I do not treat the strategy of war lightly.

Maria: *(From the catwalk)* No, the mistress has to go, she is clearly disrespecting the wife of the President, even if the President is corrupt, we will not let her corrupt the office.

Bolivar: Maria Lionza says the mistress's glamour clearly outshines her virtue, and she is sabotaging Venezuela's families.

Chavez: Understood, sir.

Bolivar: I'm proud of you Chavez. Light me a candle with a glass of red wine and talk (pray) to me. Vaya con Dios entonces— Te bendigo. No esperes un momento mas. Adios mi hijo. (Then, go with God— You have my blessings— Do not wait another moment. Goodby my son)

Chavez: Venezuela thanks you. My children and their grandchildren thank you. (*He bows respectfully*).

Maria Lionza throws two white roses to Chavez and Bolivar from the catwalk.

Maria: Know that I love you both dearly, and despite the blood on your hands, I deeply respect your courage.

Marion: I believe that the great cacique Tamanaco wants to speak.

Maria: (*From the catwalk*) Tamanaco, yes, be our guest. Your words are welcome at all times.
The young drummer, Rafael, suddenly begins to convulse, grabbing his throat. He rocks back and forth, and then dissolves into the posture of a Chief Tamanaco.

Marion: Sr. Chavez, there is more. Wait. (*addressing her assistants*) It's Tamanaco, get his feathers and the cocuy.

Tamanaco slowly gets situated in the young drummer's body He grabs his throat painfully, because he died from decapitation, and speaks.

Tamanaco: Good afternoon todos. El Cacqique Tamanaco esta aqui. Bring me my hacha and Sr. Chavez.

Chavez: Here I am brother. *Marion gives Rafael/Tamanaco his cigar/*

Tamanaco: (*Embracing him with tears in his eyes, almost speechless*) We are all watching you, all of your ancestor caciques who died for you, all of the Africans who worked the agriculture and mining in this country, all of us who struggled for liberation. And none of us like watching this lucha, after so many died in vain so long ago. Hombre . . . we are surely behind you in spirit— warriors for the truth and justice we all desire and deserve for Venezuela. Take my hand and go with the power I transmit to you from the bows and arrows of a hundred Venezuelan Chiefs. Reclaim the order of our land, once and for all. Te bendigo, mi hijo Adios y vaya con Dios!

Chavez: Gracias Tamanaco. I am honored and overflowing with your 'fuerza.' *(Fuerza is the alchemical energy of strength, kundalini, prana, chi)* I will light you many green candles.

Chavez exits.

* * *

5D. SCENE with the GRINGA CECILIA and TAMANACO

The gringa, Cecilia has been curled up watching all this with dropped jaw wonder and amazement. Tamanaco approaches her and looks straight through her.

Tamanaco: This must be the Gringa. *(He examines her) Poco* suerte en amor![14] (Little luck in love) What are you doing on this land, blond one?

Gringa: My father died of cancer, and I'm interested in the way you people make medicine and spiritual healing.

Tamanaco: We have the 'mapurite.' Do you know this?

Gringa: I'm hoping to learn more about it today.

Tamanaco: The Doctor will come to explain that. I must tell you. Your father, Joseph, loves you . . . .. he hears your prayers, and he will always support you because he believes in the goodness of your heart. For this I have been sent along with him to be your protector. He asks me to watch over you.

Gringa: My father, the republican said that? I don't know what to say. I think I'm speechless for the first time in my life. Of course, I appreciate your concern and could probably use a few holy ghosts with all the crazy things I've been through.

Tamanaco: I will protect you, and although you have not had the opportunity for true love in your life, I can tell you that the universe will send you three daughters someday, they are part Indio, but they are not from these shores. I will help you find them.
They will love you like no man has ever loved you. I will protect you, and you will find happiness in your own homeland.

Gringa: You know, difficult as that is for me to understand, I really want to believe you and thank you for caring about me. You have to remember that the closest thing I have to this is Startrek on TV. *(She breaks down)* And I don't know why I'm not married. *(more tears)* Please tell my father, Joseph, I miss him so much. so so much. He was a good man, and he died a painful death to cancer. And I'll just say hello to my grandfather Florentino Diaz, while I'm at it. Hola Abuelo! *(she waves at the sky)* Te quiero mucho! I love and miss you both very much!!

Tamanaco: Cecilia. These men are watching over you, in a world where not many men could keep up with you. I will watch over you from this day on. Mi Gringa bella, the Doctor Jose Gregorio is calling, and I must go. Get yourself a green and brown necklace and I will bless it for you. Te bendigo mi hija. I will always protect you, wherever you are on the earth. We will speak again.

Gringa: OK! Bye .... that's nice. Thank you so much. Is there some place I can reach you by phone maybe? Would you like to get together next week? And you wouldn't happen to know where I can find Maria Lionza, because you just can't call anybody up on the phone around here.

Marion: Cecilia, listen to me....... Hello?

Gringa: Hello?

Marion: Let me try to explain. You see, the way this works is . . . . Tamanaco will be your protector, from now until forever. This is a moment you will never forget, even if you never make direct contact with him again. He will always be your protector. If you call him spiritually, he will be there, just like your father, your grandfather, or anyone with whom you have had a relationship. These people live in spirit, and they hear your prayers.
However, you can't call them on the phone. You understand that right?

Gringa: Yes, of course. I guess, the artist in me got carried away into some virtual holographic idea for a moment. Never mind . . . I'm fine Marion.

Marion: Are you really? Sometimes Americans have problems with this work.

Gringa: Are you kidding? This is the best theater I have ever seen in my life!

Marion: This isn't theater Cecilia . . . this is real. Now . . . Doctor Jose Gregorio Hernandez[15] will speak to you about the cancer plant after he does this spiritual operation. I'm going to do the oracion and call him. Do you think you can handle this?

Gringa: I wouldn't miss it for the world . . .

Maria: *(From the catwalk)* Ok get ready Doctor!

Marion lights up a cigar and prays over a middle-aged woman, Anita Gonzalez.

5E. SCENE - Dr. JOSE GREGORIO and ANITA GONZALEZ

Marion: "Oh unique spirit of God without beginning without end. God of the sky, Creator of the Universe, and from whose ocean I am only a drop. I invoke in your name, Dr. Jose Gregorio Hernandez to cure this suffering pilgrim, Anita Gonzalez, in the name of the Father, the Son, and the Holy Ghost. I ask that your spiritual generosity and desire to help the needy, penetrates into this creature who desires to be healthy again— Anita Gonzalez. Inspire us with your divine power, knowledge, vigor, vitality, and ability to heal. Fortify the life energy and peace in the mind of this your creature Anita Gonzalez. We pray to you, Doctor Jose Gregorio Hernandez, that you flow over this creature, Anita Gonzalez and all who suffer, with the power of love and mercy, giving us strength to resist and conquer evil." Please come to us now in the hour of our need.[16]

Manuel is already prepared— dressed in white coat and gloves. He effortlessly takes on the Doctor with a gentle jolt, and prepares to operate without anesthesia, on Anita's cancerous tumor in her breast.

Doctor (Manuel): Doctor Jose Gregorios Hernandez present to serve you. Good afternoon.

Group: Good afternoon, Doctor.

Doctor: Good afternoon, Anita.

Anita: Good afternoon, Doctor. Thank you for helping me.

Doctor: I heard your prayers. How could I not come? I am here to give you a chance to fulfill your destiny in this life. You have a husband . . . . grandchildren ....a fabulous garden, neighbors, and a library that needs you. There are still many missions for you to complete in your life, and we need you . . . and above all . . . remember. You are in the hands of God right now. As long as it will take you to recite a Padre Nuestro and tres Ave Marias is as long as this operation will take. OK? Are you ready?

She closes her eyes and recites

Padre nuestro, que estas en los cielos.
Santificado sea tu nombre
Venga a nosotros Tu reino
hagase tu voluntad aqui en la tierra
como en el cielo
El pan nuestro de cada dia Danoslo hoy
Perdona nuestras deudas, asi como snosotros
perdonamos a nuestros desudores,
y no nos dejer caer en tentacion
mas libranos de todo mal. Amen

3X— AVE MARIA

Dios te Salve Maria
Llena eres de gracia
El Señor es contigo
Bendita tu eres
Entre todas las mujeres
Y bendito sea el Fruto de tu vientre, Jesus
Santa Maria, Madre de Dios
Ruega Por nosotros, pecadores
ahoroa y en la hora
de nuestra muerte. Amen

The Doctor has indeed extracted something from Anita's breast in the time it took to say three Hail Mary's and a Padre Nuestro. He is examining it in a glass of water, while Marion holds cotton over the open wound.

> **Doctor:** I cannot tell if any of the malignancy escaped, in which case, just to be sure . . . you must drink the Mapurite Infusion'.
>
> **Anita:** How do I make that?

Gringa: Excuse me Doctor, but I have travelled over 3,000 miles to ask you that very same question, and to steal some of your time regarding this very recipe.

Doctor: Very well, Gringa .... You can write it down for two, while I patch her up. Here are the ingredients, as the mapurite is powerful, but needs certain catalysts which activate the antioxidant processes that dissolve malignant tumors and clean the blood. These combinations have been passed on to me through the spirits of Amazonian Indigenous Shamans over the years who say they have been advised by the divas of the spirit world. Wherever it comes from, the list has proven effective over my years of practice. I repeat a special jarabe, of which mapurite is the largest ingredient.... exists, and has proven to dissolve cancerous tumors and to irradicate malignancy from the blood.

Gringa: I'm ready Doctor. *She has a pencil and paper and writes.*

Doctor: OK— Besides Mapurite (relative of our Pokeweed which grows in Caribbean – scientific name Petiveria Aliacael), we have Mastuerza (Mullein), Salbia (aloe vera), Savila (sage), Sangre de Drago (dragons blood bark), Bachaco Oriental (red ant saliva), kananga water, holy water, Yin Ting, Sandria (watermelon), mentol de la India, Manteca de Raya, Manteca de un obillo negro de besugo toro (The meat of a black spot on a male sea bream fish.) *(This exact recipe was dictated to me by Jose Gregorio in spirit).* You mix it up, without heating it, and drink it seven times a day.

Gringa: Doctor, is it possible for someone who is suffering at the terminal stages of cancer to be cured with this concoction?

Doctor: Absolutely. Once the virus is arrested, it can no longer consume remaining tissue, which will automatically rebuild if it has not been completely damaged. The Medical Spiritual court is in great agreement on this ancient recipe and has healed many hopeless cases with this treatment. We highly recommend it.

Gringa: Thank you Doctor, I'm sorry I didn't meet you before my father died. He would have been very impressed with your philosophies.

Doctor: I have talked with your father several times. Why do you think I am here now to meet you? You may share this recipe with your American Doctors. I'm not sure how seriously they will take it, but I will talk with you more on the subject if you wish. I must go now. Good afternoon.

Marion begins to pray to la Reina statue alone:

Marion: "I implore the sublime influence of the Queen Maria Lionza as my protectress by the grace that God has granted her to me. To you, my powerful Queen, I deliver all my needs so that you bless me with the power and protection that will allow me to liberate all evil and to provide happiness to my patients, and that the light of God will guide me and my thoughts always. I am your admirer, my Queen, for your strength, your knowledge and your great benevolence; I ask in the name of God to irradiate my body with your holy fluidity to distance all bad thoughts," ambushes, or black magic. I seek to heal in your name, with your fuerza, and your love."[17]

Veruska takes the Gringa aside.

Veruska: Cecilia, I will help you with the remedy, because I know a little about this plant. It grows in many tropical places by different names and is a very toxic plant which must be used wisely. My aunt did cure herself of breast cancer with tea made from this "mapurite." *(Mapurite is also the word for skunk and the plant has this smell) It's* technical name is "petiveria alliacael" and I will help you follow up on this, because it should be formally researched.

Gringa: Oh, thank you Veruska. This has all been so magical, and confusing for me. But something tells me, that perhaps this plant could be used not only for cancer, but for la sida (aids) as well. I have a feeling about that . . .

5F. SCENE WITH VERUSKA

Up on the catwalk, Maria is getting ready to descend. The pilgrims become distracted by Veruska, who begins to shake, rattle, and roll, and before long she is in trance, bursting with melodic strains of her voice filing the mountain with the familiar Catholic melody of Ave Maria. The assistants rush around looking for her cape, scepter, crown, and red wine and by the last note, everything is ready.

Marion: La Reina wants to come into Veruska .... Fuerza!! Fuerza!!! Adelante diosa/reina . . ..

Maria Lionza(Veruska): Buenas Tardes mis discipulos, como estan hoy?

Manuel: We are clearly delighted to be in your audience Holy Queen.

Maria Lionza (Veruska): I am pleased to be hosting such a diverse tribe of initiates this weekend. Welcome to my palace. Do you see the natural wealth in which I live like a Queen? Can you understand why I prefer this to the civilization that destroys itself in the name of progress? Here we have preserved a doorway for you all to enter into the other world through the animas of nature and the pure vibrations of spirit. The more unconnected man becomes to Nature the more insensitive he will become to his fellow men, and the system will implode from there. This is why you are so drawn to this pilgrimage- to the mountain where you can purify and liberate your spirits from the anguish of the city. Let us all bathe together in the beauty of God's glorious sunlight.

"By sending forth your Spirit, the faithful shall be created, and you shall renew the face of the earth . . .. Holy Spirit, you fill the hearts of the faithful, and kindle in them the fire of your love" (Pentecost Alleluia[18])

Cecilia: Maria, is it really true that there were origins in the Amazon of other mother-cult societies?

Maria (Veruska): Oh yes, my grandfather found goddess figurines in the gold-mining caves of el Tocuyo, Estado Lara, where the famous San

Juans, or Don Juanes of the nature spirits live. I used to play with them when I was a child.

Cecilia: I'd like to know more about that Señora.

Maria: OK, pour me some more wine. There are many Goddess stories from our ancestry. In Estado Guarico in a cave called Batatal is a female serpent with passionate eyes, who is sometimes related to the Candomble fire serpent Mboi-tata. The Chibcha recognize a universal mother goddess, Nabusa, relating especially with wild animals, trees, and rivers, similar to my practice. There were feminine deities relating to fertitlity like Bachue, the Earth Mother divinity of vegetation and protectress of the Muisca women. The Tucuna and Jivaros Indians believe in Nungui, a feminine goddess of fertility. The Incas venerated Pachamama, who still receives offerings from Peruvian farmers.[19]
Yemaya is also connected to aquatic deities as she is the Brasilian/ Yoruban Ocean Mother who provides similar maternal blessings. Then don't forget of course the Virgin of Coromoto, who has also appeared to my father and insisted that he get baptized. They mix us up sometimes, but I have become a mythical combination of the Virgin Mary and Yara. Yara is my true god mother, half anaconda snake, half blue-eyed human. The legend insists she seduced a young Indian into her subterranean sexual waters, whose location in Yaracuy, is not far from where I was born. This very site was clearly of ancient indigenous matrilineal culture based on all the goddess queens who I channeled there.[20] And not far from there, in Nirgua, my first parish and shrine were built in 1653 after my death, to preserve my divine legacy to the spirit of Nature and all Venezuelans. It was called "Nuestra Señora Maria de la Onza de Prado de Talavera de Nivar."

Cecilia: We would be very interested to hear more about your life as an Indian princess Maria . . . Like, were you ever in love?

Anita: Señora . . . Did you really ride that "onza" animal naked?

Rosa: What kind of supernatural powers did you have when you were alive, Maria? Could you really communicate with animals?

Cecilia: How did you die? Do you miss being in a body?

Anita: Will you ever reincarnate again?

Cecilia: You can use my uterus if you want.

Rosa: Or mine too .... if it could be an immaculate conception!

Maria: I don't believe many people have asked these questions. May I have some wine please? Perhaps you would like to take a trip to my last session in 1653— August 15th— to my house in Nirgua.

Cecilia: You mean like the time tunnel?

Maria: I mean a past life that you and Veruska had with me . . ..
when I died.

Cecilia: Yes, take us there!

Maria: Musicos! Toquen los tambores por favor! (Musicians! Play the drums please!) I suggest you just get on my butterfly, and we'll fly your back. Just close your eyes. Put your mind blank . . .. and let's go . . .

Maria begins to shake. They begin to transport to another dimension. Veruska and Cecilia will shift out of their bodies to another place, where they will occupy different bodies, from a different incarnation. The sudden sound of the "cicadas" begins to vibrate from the trees. This sound permeates the journey. The real Maria descends from the catwalk.

SCENE 6 — Time tunnel choreography

The transition will be made through a musical journey, constantly accompanied by the mysterious vibratory sound of the cicada's wings. Maria Lionza has disappeared from her catwalk throne, and el Negro and Guaicaipuro remain. The choreography is a collage of images, sensations, flashbacks, and dreamlike experiences that reflect past scenes from Act I...... We see: Yara, the Virgin del Prado de la Talavera, pregnant Princess Anna Carolina and Cacqiue Guare, Don Juan y Doña Herminia De la Talavera being served by la Negra Hamurapi, Queen Isabella and King Ferdinand, Colombus, the Conquista battles between soldiers and Indians, African slaves, and Maria Lionza holding Tamanaco in her arms. This hypnotic collage of flashbacks creates a swirling spiral energy to occur on stage, taking us through time. The light finally fades on Maria & Tamanaco.

Scene 7— The Assumption— Maria Lionza's final day in Nirgua —August 15, 1653 (About 20 miles from Sortes)

This rewind of turbulence shifts the scene to a mystical fairy land, an indoor/outdoor jungle altar, high on a rain forest mountain, next to a natural spring and reservoir. When the lights come up, we feel like we have arrived in an overgrown paradise. Marion's present-day team appears as pre-incarnated Caquetios tribal members preparing the temple altar, flashed back to a Shangri-la existence deep in the rainforest. These Caquetios Indians have escaped the domination of the Spanish ruling class in the Seventeenth Century, under the protection of Maria on her sacred land. The scene opens as Maria enters as an old woman (as the same actress on the catwalk), mounted on the back of her danta/ onza/ tapir. She painfully dismounts. The sound of the cicadas' fades.

Maria Lionza: Oh, I'm just getting too old for this. Where are the sisters? Jazmin, Yarita, help me! Oh, Goddess mia. My mother warned me about this hermit life in my better years. Thank Goddess for you my sweet onza— my namesake— my flying angel. Too bad you can't cook. Anything has to be better than those two young nuns that gave up monastery life to live with me. They are great fun ... But they can't even boil water. And now they've discovered those goodlooking boys!! I'll never eat again ...

(Cecilia as) Jazmin and (Veruska as) Yarita arrive with two handsome Indian young men, all carrying baskets laden with fruits, vegetables, and herbs.

Jazmin (Gringa as): Maria, where have you been? We expected you yesterday!

Yarita (Varuska as): We were so worried about you.

Jazmin: It's a miracle you made it. Let us help you. You look exhausted.

Yarita: How was the Virgin of Coromoto? Did you see her?

Maria: Yes, I saw her, it's Mary all right— the only difference is that she hasn't aged a day since I last saw her on my first hour of birth sixty-three years ago. There are certain advantages to living in spirit girls. I don't know how they do it, but I'm going to find out. Her skin just seems to get younger.

Jazmin: Maybe that's because she's a virgin.

Maria: Excuse me Jazmin, but unfortunately, I still qualify for the same status . . . Oh well, they did build her a beautiful statue, right there where I was born in the river— 63 years ago. So, any visitors while I was gone?

Yarita: There are several dozen pilgrims waiting for you tonight . . . . they are at the foot of the mountain, and I said I would light a fire if you were willing to hold court

Maria: Of course we're holding court. Light the fire. What's for dinner? And where's my snake? Have you been feeding her the barley?

Yarita: Yes Maria, she's fine, and look how much she misses you. *(she takes the snake from her perch on a tree branch)* I'm going to check on our new cooks. I have no idea what they are making.

Maria: Make sure there's no meat Yarita!!

Jazmin: Maria, look what we found in the river this time— all these little clay goddess figurines.

Maria: I have dozens of those. I told you that this is a sacred, pre- historic mother goddess site which sources the Guanare river, which also connects with the Yaracuy and my moutain of Sortes in Chivicoa to the southwest. You are the only white person who knows about this place Jazmin, and it's only because you were a nun that I trust you, and that's the way I want to keep it.

Jazmin: What about that Spanish soldier, who was in love with you? Wasn't he a white man?

Maria: Fernando.... yes... he wanted me........ a Spanish count, with stars in his eyes for property in Venezuela by marrying into my mother's bloodline. The greed comes with the blue blood. Yes, I was in love, but I knew the sacrifice would sabotage my spiritual destiny and Venezuela's. He bribed my sister one day to lead him to my home in Sortes. But he was ambushed and killed by local Indians who knew that no Europeans were permitted on my sacred land.[21] I wept for him for weeks. I was so unhappy. I had written him in Spain telling him to forget me, that I had chosen another path, but his ambition drove him blindly, to his demise. Somehow, I don't believe it was love. From that day on I knew I would always be a virgin, dedicated to Jesus Christ, Father Sky and Mother Earth, and all her children. Loving and preserving endangered flora, fauna, and humanity is the most important thing I can do for Venezuela. On this sacred land I have studied plants and their remedies, the stars, the cycles of the moon, the habits of insects— I talk to birds and fish, monkeys, and my onzas, to my Don Juans and the spirits of the trees and the rivers. I am a happy woman, and I still can heal people. My old nursemaid, la Negra Hamurapi's great grandchildren are around me, and I watch the tribe who farms my land multiply. Except for the atrocities and pain of my Father's people, I have been blessed by divine providence with a rich metaphysical life, and a glorious natural paradise for a home. And look at this, such royal service before my very eyes.

Yarita has returned with a bottle of red wine, which always puts a twinkle in Maria's eye.

Yarita: How would you like to be remembered Maria, when we write about you in books? *(pouring her a glass)*

Maria: Well, let's see... I spent most of my life trying to help the native people and African slaves to escape the oppression of my mother's people. There were many years when they didn't trust me, but I was dedicated to creating sacred land where ancient traditions could be preserved. I did not last long in civilized society, so I can't claim much of a ladyship. But I shall always claim a spiritual connection to this country, along with Guaicaipuro, Yaracuy, Tamanaco, Yaguarin, and all the Caciques of the resistance. I include el Negro Felipe as well and the liberated slaves, la Negra Francisca, la Negra Tomasa, la Negra Matea, el Negro Primero, el Negro Miguel. And what about Jose Gregorio? I hope Rome finally gets around to beatifying him some day. What a saint! I do love him dearly. These souls and so many more have enlightened our rich Venezuelan culture through the "Tres Potencias" Trinity and our precious belief in racial peace and equality.

Maria drinks her wine.

Yarita: I think you may be talking about future spirits mi Reina.

Maria: You know at the moment my soul seems to be flying through several incarnations.

Yarita and Jazmin look at each other like they are not sure what is happening.

Jazmin: I am going to wait to light the torch to signal the pilgrims Maria, until after you've been given permission. Are you ready?

Maria: Am I ever ready?

Yarita: Here are your tobacos. Let's see. *She hands Maria a few tobacos to conjure.*

Maria makes the sign of the cross with the tobacos and begins to pray.

Maria: En el nombre de Dios Poderoso, el hijo, y el espiritu Santo, deme la fuerza, la proteccion, y la sabiduria transportar esta noche fina abajo las estrellas en esta paradiso mio, para estar disponible para los desfortunados y enfermos. Te pido en el nombre de la Virgin Maria y todo sus poderes.

(In the name of, etc., give me the strength, protection, and knowledge to transport this evening below the stars in this paradise of mine, to be available to the unfortunate and sick. I ask in the name of the Virgin Mary and all her powers.)

Maria smokes the tobacco and everybody can tell that the roads are only partially open. There is a dark warning in the cigar ashes providing enough indication to cancel the session, but Maria really wants to work and celebrate. Up on the catwalk, el Negro and Guaicaipuro look concerned.

The Mysteries of Maria Lionza

Yarita: What does it mean Maria?

Maria: It's not dangerous.

Jazmin: But Maria, you are tired from the trip. Let's make it tomorrow for the pilgrims.

Maria: Nonsense, I'm fine. Light the torch and fill my glass.

Jazmin reluctantly goes to light the torch and ring the bell, and Yarita begins to smoke a tabaco with Maria. Jazmin returns, and pours herself a glass of wine, and lights up a conjured cigar. Some of the other local natives join them, making offerings to the altar. Some of the Afro/Latino men begin to play the tambores. Women join Maria in the smoking circle, spitting into the clay pots, and murmuring prayers.

Jazmin: This sure beat monastery life any day!

El Negro addresses Guaicaipuro up on the catwalk.

El Negro: Something is not right.

Guaicaipuro: You must go down now, maybe you can clear her heart.
Maria begins to rattle and sway, taking deep breaths and dropping her cigar. Jazmin and Yarita back her up and cry over and over, until she finally goes into trance, bringing down el Negro Felipe into her body.

Yarita & Jazmin: Fuerza para la materia, proteccion, luz, y evolution!!

Felipe: Buenas Noches todos. What a beautiful evening you have arranged here for us tonight. Unfortunately, I am really in the mood to party with Maria, but I can tell that she is not strong enough to hold court this evening.

Jazmin: Oh no . . . .

Felipe: Mis hijas, she is very sick. Her time has come. I will bless the altar and standby should you need me.

Yarita: Oh Negro, I suspect it's her heart.

Jazmin: I knew she shouldn't have made that trip alone to Guare.

Negro: Guaicaipuro has something to tell you and then we must call off the session.

Jazmin: What's wrong? What's going on?

Yarita begins to shake, and Guaicaipuro descends into her body.

Jazmin: We've got to call Maria down to earth; she can't take this fuerza.

Guaicaipuro: Wait a minute. I must tell you that we are making a path for Maria, to deliver her to the angels and archangels. She is almost ready to go. El Negro and I will take care of her. We have been waiting for her. Now it is time. Make her as comfortable as possible . . . . She is about to make the Assumption. Bring her down into her body now so she can pass over consciously.

Jazmin: *(Panicking)* Oh no Dios mio!! OK... I call Maria Lionza to the earth. Bring this creature to the earth. Now, please, in the name of God Almighty. A Tierra!!! Por Favor!! A Tierra!

Maria is weak and has difficulty coming back this time. Yarita returns to her body and Guaicaipuro leaves. The locals have made her a bed of leaves in front of the altar, and they gently lay her down. The energy required to bring down spirit has jolted her heart.

Jazmin: Please talk to us Maria . . . where are you? Get me some holy water.

Yarita: Please speak, Maria . . . It's Yarita and Jazmin, sus hijas!! Wake up Maria!! Chicos, toquen los tambores por favor!!

The boys start to play the drums, and Maria barely revives.

Maria: Well girls, I guess this is it. We've had some pretty miraculous experiences together out here in the jungle. My only regret is that you didn't learn how to cook better. Can I have my wine please?

Jazmin: Don't make jokes at a time like this Maria! Please don't leave us.

Maria: I will always be with you. You can always find me, because I've taught you all the prayers myself. I must continue my work in spirit now. Bring me my snake and my onza and let me rise. *(Jazmin gets the snake, Yarita brings in the onza, and Maria insists upon mounting the onza with her snake around her neck, lying on her belly)* I can see el Negro and Guaicaipuro waiting for me, and all the angels. Yes, this will be a grand reunion. Jazmin, I want you to ask one of those Friars to paint a picture of el Negro, Guaicaipuro and myself and call it Los Tres Poderosos. This will be the Trinity; you remember us by. You can hang it over the fireplace. This will really make me happy.

Yarita: *Jazmin and Yarita are weeping.* Please Maria, this is crazy. Just rest, you will be fine in the morning.

Maria: No, open the door. I must go now, my sisters. I can smell the roses, I can hear the music, and I see the light .... and I love you. Always say the rosary for me .... I will be there for you always. *The onza walks her outside and then ... leaps into the air, flying towards heaven) Jazmin and Yarita are speechless reaching after her with their rosaries. Music pours out of the sky which lights up majestically upon her Assumption, and butterflies seem to come from everywhere.* **Angels appear** singing a short libretto:

**"May you be blessed my daughter by God Most
High, beyond all women on earth. (Judith 13:23)
The trust you have shown shall not pass from the
memories of men but shall ever remind them of
the power of the mother Goddess. (Judith 13:25)
Glory be to the Father, and to the Son and to the holy
mother. As it was in the beginning, is now, and ever shall be
. World without end. Amen"**[22]

BLACKOUT

Scene 8 — The Coronation— October 12, 1995
— La Montana de Sortes—
Dia de la Raza and Maria Lionza's Birthday
A Celebration of Love and Wisdom

Scene 8a— Fiesta spirit at the Altar Mayor on the mountain of Sortes.

A fully dressed statue of Maria Lionza in pure white is presented in the altar mayor (without her crown). October 12, Maria Lionza's Birthday and The Day of the Races, is one of the year's biggest fiestas on the mountain of Sortes in Venezuela. The three powers sit above on the catwalk with great dignity. Salsa music is playing live in front of the Riverside entrance near the Altar Mayor. People are praying, making promises and offerings, lighting candles, and smoking tabacos. Others are dancing in the river, cooking over fires, and children play. There is fire on the dance floor in front of the Altar Mayor where three couples are dancing skillfully. They spin, lift, twist, pretzel, dip, and step off the ground in an exciting, opening salsa choreography. Devotees don't seem to be disturbed by this 'rumba' because it is El Dia de la Raza, when the magic of all the races mixes to celebrate Venezuela and its miraculous hybrid culture.

When the song ends, there is a fanfare which brings out the moving shrine and statue of Maria Lionza, which will then be carried all the way up to her grotto at the top of the mountain, followed by 'pelegrinos con promesas' (pilgrims with promises). They will accompany the Holy Queen to the Coronation. Three mediums are dressed as el Negro Felipe (Manuel), Maria Lionza (Veruska), and el Cacique Guaicaipuro (Marion), and they will lead the procession. **The pilgrims** *begin to* **sing** *as they cross the bridge and walk in solemn procession to celebrate her birthday high atop her Mountain of Sortes at her Royal Portal and the "Palace of Coronation."*

Tribute to the Reina

"Eres la misma ternura	*You have the same tenderness,*
Eres quietude y cancion	*The same quietness and song*
Eres esperanza y amor	*You are hope and love*
Porque eres la luz que brilla en los ojos	*Because you are the light that makes the eyes shine*

de un fulano que espera tu bendicione.	*Of a guy waiting for your blessing*
Porque te abre cada mano para recibir	*Because you open each hand to receive*
tu esplendor que ilumine esperanzas,	*Your splendor which brightens hopes*
y ammare su corazon	*and anchors the heart . . ..*
Te porte cosas bellas con este canto	*I bring you beautiful things with this song*
Cosas que se oyen al ritmo de estrellas en quebradas	*Things that hear the star's rhythms in the hills*
de aguas alegres y cristalinas	*of happy and crystalline waters.*
Dichosas y cantarinas—	*Sayings and songs that come from the jungle*
se va metiendo en la selva	
en este paradiso de Yaracuy	*Of this Yaracuyan paradise.*
Del corral de mis ensuenos eres tu mi portadora	*From the corral of my daydreams, you are the carrier*
trabajando por nuestras madres	*working for our mothers . . ..*
mano de mi mandador	*hand of my maker . . .*
Eres la soga tendida que va enlazando luceros	*You are the rope that connects the bright lights,*
Eres la lampara prendida que luminan mis senderos	*You are the lamp that illuminates my paths . . ..*
Senderos que tu trillaste	*Paths, that you plowed . . ..*
Los senderos de mis vida	*Paths of my life.*

CHORUS

En la Montana Maria Lionza, en sus alturas	*In ML's Mountain, in her high altars*
Eres su Reina, de sus cosechas, de sus montanas de su splendor/	*is the queen of your crops and your abundant mountains*
Mysterios encanto que va siguiendo empostaduras	*Mysterious enchantment that follows*
Cosas que murmura el ritmo del rio en un dulce canto	*the overgrown things that murmur the rhythm of the sweet singing river.*

REPEAT Chorus

End: En la Montana llena de paz, coges de amor y ternura." 2X	*En the mountain filled with peace, one gets love and tenderness 2X*

(transcribed and translated from cassette tape)

Scene 8b— Soliloquy

The company exits the stage.
A solo pilgrim (who played the poet street prophet in the beginning) lights a small candle in front of a small bust of Maria which sits on a rock on the path. He prays with his bottle of rum:

> **Poet/Prophet:** "Who are you, Maria? Where did your accent come from? Are you maybe the girl that was coveted by the adventurous men who fled from the Criolle King and made her home in nature's earth? Are you the Queen of the water? . . . the one from the clouds and mysteries that another people loved, from a farther riverbank? I know nothing of legends . . . My love just loves you purely— you are the grace of the people— After the Immaculate, you are the one. I know this from the beginning of time. You are my Queen."

(transcribed from poetry on cassette)

The Mysteries of Maria Lionza

8c— Palace of the Coronation

The lights come up, and we are in front of Maria's Royal Altar at the summit of the mountain. The company enters and places the statue of Maria in the grotto altar. They all stand in front of the statue, and each recites a different line of the following poem:

"Maria—You are the one who perfumes the night,
who nurtures the crops,
who tunes the guitar ...
You give moonlight to the lemon trees
and make the rivers flow ...
You who gives water, and humidifies the lips of the thirsty ...
You who gives strength to men ...
You who makes the wheat grow from the ground ...
You who sweetens the breast of women so that the babies can
feel maternal tenderness with their milk ...
I have felt you like a lover on my chest,
I have lived in your blood, and slept in your bones ...
My eyes have learned from your enchantments in the hills ...
Your beautiful green hills, Maria, are surrounded by dreams ...
There can only be heard the voice of silence,
spelling marvels to the beat of the wind.
When I arrived at your portal,

How beautiful you appeared to me
You dress with fragrances that lift my soul ...

How strange your green eyes ...
What a river of light emerges from your body ...
What words emerge from your lips, so wet with feelings ...
The glow of the ring at your waist ...
Such flowers in your hair ...
Never in my years of maturity have I seen beauty so perfect ...
You are the queen of the fertile mountains and the robust trees,
of enchanted and perfumed flowers,

reminding us of your spiritual beauty.
Mother of millions of believers in our villages,
growing in influence every day . . .
So great and eternal like the natural power of the star king
You materialize as the mother of the seeds . . .
Queen of the mountainous parks,
of the fertile jungles,
of the black beaches and the singing waters.
Mother Goddess of the aboriginal skies, come down to us now . . .
We are waiting for you to manifest the beauty of nature in your
physical presence once again on this your sacred birthday
— Our Dia de la Raza!"

(transcribed and translated from poetry on cassette tape)

The three mediums stand in front of the altar holding hands. The tambores begin. The wind is blowing, and the 'materia' (mediums) are collecting fuerza from the miraculous vortex in which they stand. Shortly all three of them transport in a splendidly synchronistic moment of mystery.

El Negro (Manuel): Buenas Noches todos. Me alegre estar aqui para honorar la Reina esta noche, porque, como siempre, este ritual es como un festival de amor. And I still put rum second to love! (Good evening everybody. I'm happy to be here to honor the Queen this evening, because, as always, this ritual is like a festival of love.)

Guacaipuro (Marion): Y yo tambien tengo el argullo de estar parte de nuestra celebracion de la Trinidad de las Razas con la Madre como nuestra Reina. She has taught me to have patience with white people over the years. And I also am proud to be part of this celebration of the three races with the Mother as our Queen.

Maria (Veruska): Buenas noches todos. Maria Lionza bendice a todos los presentes en el nombre del Padre . . . yo ofrezco proteccion espiritual para todos. Pido a todos orar "como homenaje a las fuerzas de la Naturaleza, el aire, el agua, la tierra y el fuego, elevando la oracion hasta el Padre Creador del Universo que les permitia tener viento como un coro eterno." (Good evening, everybody. Maria Lionza blesses everybody present in the name of the Father and offers spiritual protection for all. I ask that you all pray, in honor of the forces of Nature, the air, the water, the earth, and the fire; elevating the prayer to the Father, Creator of the Universe, allowing the wind to sound like an eternal chorus.)

Negro: "Who is this arising like the dawn, fair as the moon, resplendent as the sun?" (Song 6:10)

Guaicaipuro: "Like the rainbow gleaming against brilliant clouds, like blossoms in the days of spring." (Ecclesiastes 50: 7,8)

Maria: *She sings*

"I am the rose of Sharon,	
I am the lily of the valleys."	
"My throne is in a pillar of clouds,	(Song 2:1)
and for eternity I shall remain."	
"Approach me, you who desire me,	(Eccles 24:4, 9)
and take your fill of my fruits."	
I am like a vine putting out graceful shoots,	(Eccles 24:19)
my blossoms are sweeter than honey. "And	(Eccles 24: 17,20)
now my children listen to me;	
listen to instruction and learn to be wise."	(Prov 8: 32,33)
"Happy are those who keep my ways,	
who day after day, watch at my gates." "For	
those who find me find life,	(Prov 8: 34, 35)
and win favor from the Lord."[23]	(Prov 8: 36)

Negro Felipe and Guaicaipuro ceremoniously lift the crown and hold it above Maria Lionza's (Veruska) head. They recite:

Felipe: Oh God, Divine Almighty Power of Heaven, Crown of the Faithful

"Bless this crown, we beseech thee, and so sanctify our servant, Maria Lionza upon whose head this day you do place it, for a sign of royal majesty, that she may be filled by your abundant grace, with all queenly virtues, through God, Amen."[24]

Guacaipuro: "God (Father sky) crowns you with a halo of glory and righteousness, that having a right faith and abundant fruit of good works, you may obtain the crown of an everlasting kingdom, By the gift of (the ancient Mother Goddess,) whose kingdom endures forever." (Taken from the formal Coronation of Queen Elizabeth II by the Archbishop of Canterbury and slightly rearranged to serve my purposes.)

The crown is placed. The crowd applauds.

Negro Felipe: We honor you Maria Lionza because we feel your love, we need your love, and we never want to be far from your love.

Guacaipuro: Maria, until eternity you are Venezuela's Queen/Angel, for the halo of your love can only be celebrated with such a Royal Crown for a true Queen of Heaven and Earth.

Maria: It is from my heart that I bless each of you tonight for celebrating El Dia de la Raza with me on my birthday, in a true spirit of sincere humanitarian love. Oh, my dear children, Could the mystery be, that our blood all runs together deep in the veins of Mother Earth, and from her same womb we all come and go? I ask you this in the spirit of peace. Yes . . . we are all brothers and sisters, and I will gladly lay my blessing down on anyone who dedicates themselves to that world family. So, fill my glass, and show me a real Coronation party!!!!

Felipe: Feliz Cumpleanos mi hermana! Care for some rum?

Maria: Negro! Five hundred years, and you still can't remember my drink! You are the rum drinker!

Guaicaipuro: Ah yes, mi Reina....... *(pouring Maria a glass of red wine)*
He remembers your birthday, and that's good for Venezuela.

Happy Dia de la Raza!!

There is a reprise of Ruben Blades salsa song about the Montana de Sortes; and once again there is a multi-level fiesta/ritual that becomes the song and dance FINALE of the Mysteries of Maria. Some dance, some pray, some talk to the spirits, others drink, most are looking for happiness, and they all sing as passionately as they can on this Holy Birthday of the (mixed) Races. As the new moon reveals itself, the poet/prophet returns for his final delivery holding a candle. He stands in the foreground to the side and recites-

Poet/prophet:

**"Sortes, your plants are moved by the seasons ...
Down the rocks of the Yaracuy, slide the memories of the water ...
That's how I reconstruct the Mysteries of Maria in my heart,
along with the whispering wind,
which always flies through the air, like a spiritual gust of eternity ....."**

(transcribed and translated from poetry on cassette tape)

THE END

Cecilia Anne Gruessing, M.A.

BIBLIOGRAPHY

The Mysteries of Maria Lionza

Acts 1 & 2

Ashton, Joan, Mother of All Nations, Harper and Rowe, SF, 1989

Berecht, Fatima, Editor, Taino, Pre-Columbian Art and Culture from The Carribean, The Monacelli Press, Inc. NY 1997

Blanco, Celia, Manual EsotericoU, Representaciones Loga, Miranda, Venezuela, 1988

Carroll, Michael, P., The Cult of the Virgin Mary, Princeton University Press, 1986

Christian, William A., Local Religion in Sixteenth Century Spain, Princeton University Press, 1981

Cunneen, Sally, In Search of Mary, Ballentine Books, N.Y., 1996

Durham, Michael S., Miracles of Mary, Harpers, SF, 1995

Fox, Mathew, Editor, Hildegard of Bingen's Book of Divine Works, Bear & Co. Santa Fe, N. Mexico, 1987

Hebert, Albert, The Tears of Mary and Fatima, Why? - Albert Hebert S.M.; Paulina, La, 1983

Marsland, William and Amy, Venezuela Through Its History, Thomas Crowell Co., N.Y., 1954

Mervin, Sabrina & Prunhuber, Carol, Women-Around the World and Through the Ages, Atomium Books, Wilmington, DE, 1990

Moreno, Santiago de Jesus Rodriguez, Biografia y Origen de su Majestad Reina Maria Lionza, Editorial Los Llanos, San Juan de los Morrows, Guarico, Venezuela, 1979

Moron, Guilliermo, A History of Venezuela, Roy Publishers, NY, 1963

Oviedo y Banos, Don Jose, The Conquest and Settlement of Venezuela,

University of California Press, Berkley/La/London, 1987

Perottet,Tony, Editor, Venezuela, APA Publications, Singapore, 1994

Pollak-Eltz, Maria Lionza, Mito y Culto Venezolano, Universidad Catolica Andres Bello, Caracas, 1985

Salazar, Homero, Yara; El Libro Del Siglo: La Historia de Maria Lionza, Editorial El Aragueno, CA, 1988

Tavard, George, The Thousand Faces of the Virgin Mary, The Liturgical Press, Collegeville, Minn., 1996

Warner, Maria, Alone of All Her Sex, Vintage Books, NY, 1983

Weber, Christian Lore, Circle of Mysteries, Yes International Publishers, St. Paul, Minn. 1995

Wilbert, Johannes, Editor, Encyclopedia of World Cultures, South America, Vol. VII, GK Hall and Co., Boston, Mass.

BIBLIOGRAPHY

The Mysteries of Maria Lionza

ACT 3

Alvarez, Manuel Diaz, El Medico de Los Pobres— Dr. Jose Gregorio Hernandez, Ediciones Paulinas, Caracas, Venezuela, 1991

Blanco, Celia, Manuel Esoterico, Representaciones Loga, C.A., Miranda Venezuela, 1988

Castellanos, Iris, Maisanta— En Caballo de Hierro, Fuentes Editores, Caracas, 1992

Maria Lionza y Su Corte Celestial, LibroOferta, Caracas, Venezuela, 1990

McMahon, Rev. Msgr John A, Censor Librorum, Scriptural Rosary, Christianica Center, Chicago, 1966

Montoya, Roberto Hernandez, The Cult of Venus in Venezuela, http://www.

analitica.com/bitblio/rhernand/venus-i.htm

Moreno, Santiago de Jesus Rodriguez, Biografia y Origen de su Majestad Reina Maria Lionza, Editorial Los Llanos, Guarico, Venezuela, 1979

Pollak-Eltz, Angelina, Maria Lionza, Mito y Culto Venezolano, Universidad Catolica Andres Bello, Caracas, Venezuela, 1985 Rivero, Armando, Maria Lionza— La Diosa del Amor y de la Fortuna, Producciones David-River, Caracas, Venezuela.

Salazar, Homero, Yara, El Libro del Siglo, La Historia de Maria Lionza, Editorial El Aragueno, C.A., 1988

Simpson, George Eaton, Black Religions in the New World, Columbia University Press, NewYork, 1978

ENDNOTES

The Mysteries of Maria Lionza

Acts 1 & 2

1 Wilbert, J., Encyclopedia of World Cultures, Vol 7, pg. 340

2 Yara is a Pre-Columbian Goddess of the Waters from the Tupari culture who is half woman and half anaconda/snake, who lives in the underworld and brings benevolence, fertility, and healing to tribal members through the shaman. She represents the ancient "Earth Mother" who actually is half animal.

3 Parintins.com-Toadas: Caprichoso 98: Canto daYara

4 NOVA Online/Warriors of the Amazon/The Last Shaman (4)

5 Bercht, Fatima, Taino, Pre-Columbian Art and Culture from the Caribbean, pg 41

6 World Religions, SA Indians, pg 1021

7 Tamanaco was a great Venezuelan Indian Chief in the 16th century. He is a poetic anachronism in this context because I am featuring him because he is my personal protector who, among many, lost his life for his people.

8 Christian, W., Local Religion in 16th Century Spain, pg 91 & 111— I have tracked down this hermitage, outside of Toledo, Spain where the principal character of this story, Maria Lionza, draws lineage, based on her mother and father's same name— (The Virgin) del Prado de la Talavera de la Reina.

9 precitool.com.mx/talavera.htm— (translation from Spanish) "At the end of the 13th century the Arabs introduced to Spain, through Majorca, a special white, antique ceramic glaze with beautiful ornate designs, which became famous near Toledo in the Cathedral work, and later was brought around 1550 to America by the Dominican monks of Talavera de la Reina.

10 Christian, W., pg. 113

11 catholicchurch.org/iglesia/maria/cantos.htm

12 Christian, pg 100. The water at this particular shrine had curative properties

and came from an underground sulphur hot springs below the hermitage which arrived with an apparition of the virign in the 16th century.

13 Adams, Henry, Mont Saint Michel and Chartres,

14 Christian, pg 82 "The poor or the powerless have the visions, and the eventual imposition of their truth upon the town authorities is a sure way of showing that Mary or the saint comes to serve everybody; that the bond set up between the saint and the town is also a direct bond between the saint and each person of the town, beginning with the powerless."

15 Hoye, Daniel, Monsignor, Household Blessings and Prayers, pg 362

16 www.udayton.edu/mary/resources/engseven.html

17 Herbert, A., The Tears of Mary-and Fatima Why?, pg 32

18 Moreno, Chapter One—This book is a channeled account, from Maria Lionza herself of her life story. It also conflates with the stories she personally told me of her Mother and Father.

19 Warner, pg 262

20 Fox, Mathew, Hildegard of Bingen's Book of Divine Works, pg 379

21 Marsland, Venezuela Through It's History, pg 55— "The encomendero won the right to the services of the Indians in exchange for certain benefits he was supposed to provide. According to the laws, he had to protect the Indians from injustice, make them live in villages and observe civilized social mores governing family life. He was ordered to instruct them in the Christian religion, organize domestic government under the authority of the Indian chief, direct their work and destroy all savage habits and inclinations."
**European Voyages of Exploration: Latin America— www.acs.ucalgary.ca/HIST/tutor/ervoya/Latin.html"
The leader and main investor of an expedition would have the title of "captain" and was invariably an important encomendro; a member or former member of a colonial municipal council, a senior settler in the area, a wealthy man, or a nobleman."

22 The Yaracuy River in Barquisimetro, Venezuela is where Maria Lionza's Sacred National Reserve is for the practice of her cult in present day.

23 Marsland, pg 54—The European smallpox wiped out two thirds of the indigenous population. "When the plague began to diminish in 1581, the

The Mysteries of Maria Lionza

decimated indians ceased to give the Spaniards serious trouble."

24 There are different legends about Maria Lionza's parents, but all agree that whichever parent was Indian, knew that the tribe would reject the child because of "clear eyes".

25 There was a serious drought in Venezuela in the early 1590's along with the plague, which increased the arrival of African slaves to do work in the fields that the Indians could not do.

26 Moreno, pg 14— La Negra Haimarupi was the actual Black nursemaid of Princess Carolina, and Maria Lionza who arrived around the same time as the family did in the 1570s and had been thoroughly indoctrinated into the Catholic Church.

27 Songs to Mary/Bride of God;Anima Mariae http://cgi.geocities.com/Athens

28 Marian Titles in the Popular Religiosity of Latin America; www.udayton.edu/ mary/resources/engseven.

29 Cuneen, S., In Search of Mar y, pg 61

30 Advocaciones Marianas— Venezuela; aciprensa.com/advvenez.htm— (translated from Spanish) "The 7 of October 1944, Pope Pio XII declared the Virgin of Coromoto the Patron of the Republic of Venezuela and her coronation was celebrated in 1952, three centuries after her apparition.

31 Cuneen, pg 275

32 http://catholic.net/RCC/Indices/Inspirations/mass-parallel.txt— Ordinary of the Tridentine Mass— 1962Mervin, Sabrina and Prunhuber, Carol, Women Around the World And Through the Ages— pg 199

33 http://lcweb2.loc.gov/cgi-bin/query/r?frd/cstdy:@field(DOCID+es0017)— SPAIN:The Golden Age "Once Islamic Spain had ceased to exist, attention turned to the internal threat posed by hundreds of thousands of Muslims living in the recently incorporated Granada. 'Spanish society drove itself', historian J.H. Elliot writes, 'on a ruthless, ultimately self-defeating quest for an unattainable purity."

34 http://encarta.msn.com/index/conciseindex/5b/o5b68000.ht m —

Torquemada, Tomas de

35 http://www.acs.ucalgary.ca/HIST/tutor/ervoya/columbus.html— European Voyages of Exploration

36 Bercht, F., pg 171

37 http://www.elmbavenez-us.org/cultural/fiestas.html— "This is a carnivalesque celebration, in which devils with many horns and different human or animal faces parade around the town to arrive at the main church. These devils are paying penance, and the amount of horns show the many sins they are paying for. Just in the same way as this celebration took place in 16th century Spain, so it was taken to its colonies."

38 http://www.uhhp.com/h9.html— King Ferdinand's letter to the Arawak/Taino (letter was reprinted in one of Bartoleme de las Casas)

39 Moron, G., A Histor y of Venezuela, pg 35— Fray Bartolome de las Casas (1474-1566) was a Spanish missionary and historian known as the Apostle of the Indians who was the first to criticize the oppression of Native Americans by their European conquerors. He gained royal permission to colonise the whole Venezuelan coast with farmers brought from Castille, and by means of peaceful persuasion he hoped to convert and pacify the natives. The task was to protect the Indians from slavery and other ill-treatment. But the monastery was wiped out by the Indians in 1520.

40 Blanco, C., pg 489— Padre Nectorio Maria was another famous Spanish Franciscan monk who wrote about Indigenous Venezuela

41 http://cgi.geocities.com/Athens/Acropolis/5743/marysong.html

42 Oviedo y Banos— Chapter VII

43 Ibid, pg 227

44 Blanco, C., pg 119— El Negro Felipe was an Afro-Cuban slave who followed in the footsteps of Negro Miguel around 1550 as a liberator. He forms part of the trinity of Maria Lionza, and graces every Espiritista altar in Venezuela with his healing presence.

45 Oviedo y Banos, pg 226— Tapia was a soldier whose historical claim to fame as an associate of Pedro Alonzo, was to seize an abandoned Indian baby lying on a beach, and grasping her by the foot he submerged and drowned her in the waters saying "I baptize you in the name of the Father, the Son, and the Holy

Spirit."

46 Ibid, pg 200

47 Lyrics come from personally recorded tambor sessions in the jungle pueblo where I lived (Birongo, Ven)

48 Cuneen, pg 148

49 Oviedo y Banos, pg 227

50 Tavard, pg 161

51 Carroll, M.— Carrol makes a lot of psychological analysis about the "machismo" complex from Spain and Italy. What I have gleamed from the Spanish Conquista machismo is that so many strong Indians and Slaves who resisted domination who were murdered, left a lot of submissive male genes around to be submissive to the crown and the white European male with all his organized control issues.

ENDNOTES

The Mysteries of Maria Lionza

Act 3

1 Rivero, pg 42 (A standard prayer to Maria Lionza)

2 'Mapurite' means skunk in Spanish and is one of many vernacular names used for this tropical miracle plant, formally called 'Petiverea Alliacael.' I followed three people who were using this plant as a cure for cancer in Venezuela and became convinced that it worked.

3 Castellanos, Iris, Maisanta, en caballo de hierro, pg 17— discusses Hugo Chavez Frias, as the commander in Chief of the Armed Forces, also great grandson of Pedro Perez Delgado, or "Maisanta", El ultimo hombre a caballo", who opposed Juan Vicente Gomez in the late twenties.

4 Ibid, pg 6

5 Robeto Hernandez Montoya, The cult of Venus in Venezuela, pg 2— http://www.analitica.com/bitblio/rhernand/venus-i.htm

6   Ibid, pg 1

7   La Reina Maria Lionza y Su Corte Celestial, pg43

8   Pollak-Eltz, Angelina, pg 71— "Los peregrinos prosiguen su camino y llegan al primer portal, donde depositan ofrendas y encienden algunas velas. Desde aqui empieza la subida; antes de llegar al Palacio de la Coronacion, hay que llevar a cabo el mismo ritual en cada portal. Llegados a la "escalera" (otro nombre del Palacio de la Coronacion) preparan el campanento y luego rinden homenaje a la Reina."

9   La Reina Maria Lionza y Su Corte Celestial, pg 45

10 Rivero, pg 53

11 A "Despojo" is a brujeria term for banishing darkness from a person, place, or thing. This can be done with special baths that are concocted (with ammonia as a main ingredient), gunpowder rings, house cleaning, special candle trabajos, or anything that distances and banishes the negativity hindering some process.

12 The cicadas have a mysterious sound in summer, and is considered a romantic sign since the male creates this sound for the female by vibrating two flaps in his throat. This sound is considered auspicious for spiritual work in Venezuela. The ancient Greeks also highly appreciated the love song of the 5 eyed cicada.

13 Simpson, George, pg 164-65 "This cult originated in the mountains of Sortes and in the state of Yaracuy during the colonial period in an area where African, American Indian, and European cultural elements were intermingled. In its original form, it was based on veneration of natural forces and on the spirits which inhabitied rivers, caverns, and the forest . . . . In recent years, the migration of Cuban and Trinidadians to Venezuela hs introduced a number of African spirits, and in particular the SEVEN AFRICAN POWERS. This includes, Obtala, Orula, Yemaya, Oshun,

Ogun, Chango, Elegua. The cult of Maria Lionza does not approve of Santerian animal sacrifice on her sacred land, and there is conflict in this arena.

14 TAMANACO, the great Indian Chief of Venezuela lived in the mid 1500s. I

met him in spirit in the back room of a Perfumeria in Catia in 1991. He was the first Venezuelan spirit with whom I'd ever conversed in this practice, and he immediately offered to be my protector. He has manifested himself to me physically during the writing of this project. As part of the Corte India, one lights a green candle to invoke him.

15 Alvarez, Manuel Diaz, El Medico De Los Pobres— Dr. Jose Gregorio Hernandez was the "Doctor of the Poor People" and lived during the turn of the century. He died tragically in a car accident in 1919. I actually interviewed him on videotape regarding the recipe for the cancer cure. Also, on videotape I have this very operation which is mentioned in the script. He worked on people for free, during his life, and in spirit. He is known all over Latin America for his altruism and is supposed to be beatified some day in Rome.

16 Blanco, Celia, pg. 484 (translated from the Spanish)

17 Ibid, pg. 103

18 Scriptural Rosary, pg. 71

19 Pollak-Eltz, pg. 28

20 Ibid, pg. 31

21 Moreno, Santiago, pg. 26-30

22 Scriptural Rosary, pg. 75

23 Ibid, pg. 78-79

24 "The Coronation of her majesty Queen Elizabeth II, June 1953"— http:// www.oremus.org/liturgy/coronation/cor1953b.html

www.ingramcontent.com/pod-product-compliance
Lightning Source LLC
Chambersburg PA
CBHW081506040426
42446CB00017B/3418